MANIFESTING
HAPPINESS

A Journal to Attract
All Good Things

FOR RIPLEY,
YOU'RE THE BEST THING
THAT EVER HAPPENED
TO ME X

MANIFESTING HAPPINESS

A Journal to Attract All Good Things

Esther McCann

Illustrated by Kerrie McNeill

DK | Penguin Random House

Editor Caroline West
Designer Joelle Wheelwright
In-house Editor Florence Ward
Senior Designer Anna Formanek
Design Assistance Isabelle Merry
Proofreader Claire Nottage
Senior Production Editor Marc Staples
Senior Production Controller Louise Minihane
Managing Editor Pete Jorgensen
Managing Art Editor Jo Connor
Publishing Director Mark Searle

Written by Esther McCann
Cover and interior illustrations Kerrie McNeill

First published in Great Britain in 2023
by Dorling Kindersley Limited
DK, One Embassy Gardens, 8 Viaduct Gardens,
London SW11 7BW

The authorised representative in the EEA is Dorling Kindersley
Verlag GmbH. Arnulfstr. 124, 80636 Munich, Germany

Design and illustration Copyright © 2023 Dorling Kindersley Limited
A Penguin Random House Company

Text copyright © Esther McCann, 2023

10 9 8 7 6 5 4 3 2 1
001-336060-July/2023

A CIP catalogue record for this book is available from the British Library.
ISBN 978-0-2416-2547-7

Printed and bound in Slovakia

For the curious
www.dk.com

MIX
Paper | Supporting
responsible forestry
FSC™ C018179

This book was made with Forest
Stewardship Council™ certified
paper – one small step in DK's
commitment to a sustainable future.
**For more information go to
www.dk.com/our-green-pledge**

CONTENTS

FIRST OF ALL,
WELCOME

Well, hey there, gorgeous soul, and welcome to *Manifesting Happiness*, a self-exploratory journey to help you create more light, love, joy, fun, and magic in your life. This isn't a gimmicky book about filling up our lives with more stuff that we think might make us feel good for five minutes, though. This is about cultivating a sense of inner peace and trust and connecting to what's going well in our lives at any given time. Happiness is here now and happiness is magnetic.

Let me tell you a little bit about myself. Once upon a time, I was anything but happy. Having lost my mother unexpectedly at 17, I went into my 20s feeling lost and depressed. I made many questionable choices during those years as I searched for what would fill the holes in my heart, but ultimately, I am thankful for my journey because it led me to this point, to finding my own "happy place." And now I feel so truly blessed to be able to hold your hand as you begin to tap into the magic that is manifesting and the magic that is you.

So, what is manifesting?

Manifesting is the energetic creation process of bringing an idea, desire, dream, feeling, or even a single thought into being. In a nutshell, your dreams become reality. What you manifest is what shows up in your life, positively or negatively, based on the thoughts, feelings, and energy you're putting out. It can be a conscious and intentional choice—the inner work we will be doing on this journey—or it can be unconsciously manifested through the vibration you're putting out, which you might be unaware of. For example, if you notice a repeating cycle in relationships, or that money flows without you even asking it to, then this is unconscious manifesting.

Why did I write this journal?

This is a journal of "being" rather than "doing": being happy, being grateful, being hopeful, being blessed, and being love. Of course, actions and seizing the day will always be a part of our journey when aligned moments arise, but essentially, it is my wish that over the next six months you'll be more focused on shifting your thoughts and feelings than taking every action under the sun. In doing so, you will shift your energy and embody what it means to become magnetic to all the blessings you desire. Manifesting isn't about the hustle, but about the ease.

TREADING CAREFULLY

A small disclaimer. I am not an advocate of toxic positivity. Yes, we're on a journey to happiness, but all emotions have a place and teach us where we are holding ourselves in resistance to our desires, as well as which parts of us need more love. What we resist and repress will only come back around asking to be loved and healed later. However, because this is a journal, the questions are generally more focused on positivity and are designed to keep steering you toward your self-worth, satisfaction, and joy.

It wouldn't be right for me to ask you potentially triggering questions that might open up cans of trauma worms, leaving you feeling helpless or vulnerable, but, if you do find you need a break, go for it! Return when you feel ready. But please do return and, if appropriate, seek the help of a medical professional.

NOW, LET'S GET STARTED

Before we get this show on the road, here I will break down the basics of manifesting, so you have a set of principles to return to—although the overarching rule is always to do what gives you the greatest happiness, peace, and contentment.

A guide to setting intentions

Intention-setting techniques should first and foremost be fun. In this book, I have included a popular manifesting technique to try at the start of each four-week cycle. These should connect you to your power, to the vision, and to the feeling, as well as help you learn to trust in the process. But at the end of the day it all comes down to you, your belief, and your energy after completing the exercise. You are the magic wand to which the Law of Attraction responds. Often, lots of questions can come up that throw some doubt or resistance into the mix. So let's clear those up now! (By the way, if you're wondering what all the manifesting terminology means, please refer to the Glossary on page 142.)

* Am I asking for too much? You can absolutely ask for more than one desire at a time. In fact, you can set as many intentions as you wish because the Universe is limitless. The only limit is the belief that we can't have it all or we're asking for too much or being greedy. It is also wise to have intentions in several different life areas because this helps you to "get off topic" if you become too focused and attached to achieving results in one area—finding Mr. or Mrs. Right, for example.

* Should I start big or small? The idea that manifestations or achievements are big or small is measured purely by the human experience and societal labels of what is regarded as "a big deal," successful, important, or rare. However, I usually recommend starting with whatever is believable for you and building faith from there. What you deem as small may feel very big to someone else; it's relative to you. You can even throw in some things you don't really care about—perhaps "it would be nice to hear from person X, but I don't really mind either way." When there is no attachment, this makes it easier for things to flow.

* I think I did it wrong, so do I need to start again? If you explore some of the intention-setting techniques in the book, you'll undoubtedly find people using different variations of the same process. All are correct if they serve the individual. Your energy and focus are a fantastic indicator of whether you are in resistance or allowing your manifestation to come through. If you're worrying that you've messed up, you're probably not in faith of the process and your power. Self-awareness is a superpower that can show what you're allowing into your life by how you feel. That beautiful sense of trust and expectancy which co-exist is evidence of being at one with your manifestation.

Understanding surrender/detachment

This is the part of manifesting that people either don't like to hear or struggle to accept. Let it go, babes. There are only so many actions you can take, only so many moves you can make before you exhaust yourself. And to be honest, forcing your way through every door and hustling your way to the bank at the expense of your well-being really isn't what manifesting is about. It certainly won't make you happy along the journey, only frustrated. In this journal we will explore what it means to embody the energy of surrendering your manifestation (see page 111).

If on your journey you find yourself in a situation where something just doesn't seem to be working out, or it isn't flowing easily and you feel as if you keep getting blocked or diverted, then this might not be your door or opportunity. In other words, it's not actually in alignment with you. If that's the case, step back. In surrendering, if it's meant for you, it will come through, but if it doesn't, you might have just spared yourself some drama. Trust and allow the Universe to deliver what will truly make you happy.

LET'S GET CLEAR FIRST!

For the Universe to deliver what we want, we must be very clear about what we are asking for in terms of desired feelings. For example, someone may wish to receive a text from an ex, but they manifest one from the wrong ex. Cringe! And yes, this does happen.

So, establishing what you don't want is a great way to understand exactly what it is that you do want—because it is usually the opposite. Use the three exercises below to gain clarity on what it is you wish to feel. You are seeking an emotion for every experience or object you hope to bring into your life.

Stage 1 Contrast: First, think about what you don't want and note this down below. Be as clear as possible here. For example, "I don't want clients who don't value me; I don't want a partner who is too busy for me; or I don't want to feel insecure." For the purpose of this exercise, it is okay to address what we don't want. Abraham Hicks calls this "contrast." Without experiencing the negative, we would not know what we do want from life instead. This helps to mold our preferences and shape our dreams. The negative allows us to have perspective on what makes us feel good. Sometimes the biggest growth and need for expansion comes from hitting rock bottom. It can take great discomfort to get us to move.

_____

_____

_____

_____

_____

_____

Stage 2 Clarity: Try to think what the opposite of the contrast points from Stage 1 would look like and write those positive desires as affirmation statements on the opposite page. Where you can, try to start with the phrase "I am" or "Thank you or." This is the most powerful way to affirm because you are speaking in the present tense and telling your subconscious that it is already real and present. Your subconscious does not know what is truth and what is not. So for the points suggested in Stage 1 you could say: "I am confident in my abilities" or "Thank you for my clients who pay on time," for example.

Stage 3 Vibration/Frequency: What feelings will you achieve from the positive statements you made in Stage 2? Pinpoint those feelings and write them down below. For instance, you may feel loved, satisfied, successful, peaceful, or secure. Your job from today will be to find ways in which you can experience those feelings in your life—perhaps by feeling love with your family and friends. This is important because your feelings are part of the magnetic vibration or frequency that you are sending out. The key to manifestation is to feel good and worthy now, even in the absence of your desire... and the rest will follow.

A WHEEL OF LIFE

This is a coaching tool designed to help you see in which areas of life you feel fulfilled and to explore what could make you feel more content in those life areas.

The wheel shown opposite covers the basics of money, career, relationships, and the body, but feel free to use the four remaining segments to insert some of the primary feelings or other manifestations you are seeking in your life. At the end of this journal, we will assess how satisfied you are in these areas to give you a quantifiable measure of how much happier you feel.

So, grab your coloring pens. For each segment, if you feel full and completely satisfied in this life area or feeling, you could color in the whole segment. If you felt 0 satisfaction, then you would leave it empty. Try to color in each segment according to how full you feel. Once you've completed your wheel, reflect on the following questions:

1. What would you like to get out of using this journal?

_____

_____

2. At this point in your journey, what do you think happiness means to you?

_____

_____

3. Where do you already feel satisfied on your wheel?

_____

_____

4. What are you ready for more of in your life?

_____

_____

Date: _____

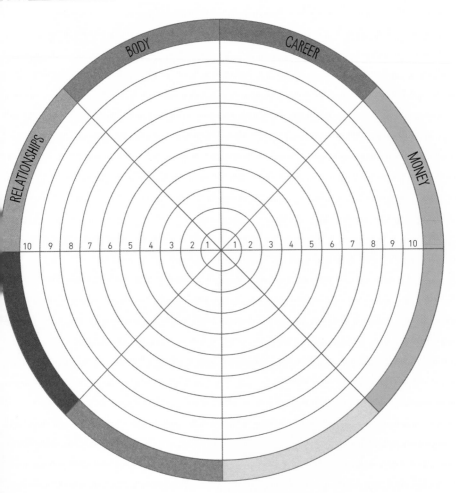

| | | | | | | | | | | | | | | | | | | |
|10|9|8|7|6|5|4|3|2|1| |1|2|3|4|5|6|7|8|9|10|

Scores:

Relationships

Body

Career

Money

HOW TO USE THIS BOOK

This book is for you to use actively because consciously creating happiness is a lifestyle. It is made up of six cycles, each of which focuses on the four weeks of a month. Every cycle begins with an intention-setting exercise, which is a tried-and-tested manifestation technique.

The idea is to set a desired intention at the start of each cycle and then to use the four weekly topics to help you do the inner work, so you can manifest your desires. Each week includes the following sections:

*Intentions:** This section looks at a specific topic, such as Energy and Gratitude in Cycle 1 and Grounding and Presence in Cycle 2. It asks you to identify the *desired feelings* you would like to nurture, answer various *power questions*, and consider the *aligned actions* you can take that week. The idea then is to maintain and embody what you have established in the Intentions section as you answer the daily prompts on the following Focus pages. You may want to make a note of your answers for the Intentions, perhaps using stickie notes so you can use these as reminders. Pop them on the bathroom mirror or somewhere you will see them regularly throughout your day.

*Focus:** Here you will be given three daily prompts to ask yourself more *power questions*, take *aligned actions*, and write *affirmations* around that week's topic. Space is provided on the pages so you can record your thoughts and feelings each day. If you need more space to do this, use a notebook to add more or even to repeat the week.

*Reflections:** Space is provided here for you to reflect on what you have learned in the last week, assess how you approached the topic, and consider how you can make changes going forward.

Each cycle includes a Success Story to show how the intention-setting exercises worked in real life for people just like you. Hopefully, these stories will inspire you and encourage you to keep going with the process. There are also inspirational quotes and reminders throughout to help you as you do the inner work, focus on cultivating happiness, and nurture your manifestation intentions.

You can start the journal at any time, at the beginning of a month, or perhaps in line with the moon cycles. Start on a day that feels powerful and exciting for you. If you miss a day, don't beat yourself up and think: "That's it, my manifestation isn't coming now." Not at all—that thought only adds resistance. Just pick up where you left off, as you can always start again.

I can feel your readiness to expand, and now we have a starting point for what you want to focus on creating in the long term, let's find your happy in the now!

Remember to do this your way! If you get to a certain week in the journal and think "This isn't what I need right now," then have a flick through and find a week that will soothe your soul or put a fire of excitement in your belly. The only rule is to choose what's right for you.

Let's start manifesting...

HAPPINESS, PEACE, AND PERSONAL POWER ARE JUST A PERSPECTIVE SHIFT AWAY.

CYCLE 1:
THE PASSAGE TO CLEAR SEEING

In our first cycle together, we are focusing on awareness and perception. As a society we are driven and guided by a sense of lack, buying into preconceived ideas of success, enjoying the instant gratification of consumerism, and obsessed with often unattainable standards of beauty. All in all, this can leave us feeling inadequate and that we are "not enough," physically, emotionally, and financially. Manifestation is essentially a game of being and it's time to break this self-defeating spell. In this cycle, you will develop an awareness of where you should place your energy going forward, while also perceiving how great both you, and many aspects of your life, already are. Manifesting happiness is the vibrational result of finding the joy that already exists in your life and recognizing all the places where contentment already resides in your heart. When you start to look at your life differently, life begins to mirror something beautiful back to you.

Let's take a look.

INTENTION-SETTING EXERCISE:
VISION BOARD

Visualization works because, as you connect to the visualized images and feelings, it tricks the subconscious mind into believing you're already experiencing that moment. Creating a vision board of what you hope to manifest programs you to go forth and create love, success, freedom, or any other desire, with your energy and actions.

1. Create your board digitally with a collage tool or use a corkboard. Make a few separate boards for different life areas or use one board to cover all goals.

2. The Law of Attraction works on the basis that like attracts like, so gratitude is an important factor. Include pictures of places, people, or things you love on your board—it should make you feel good NOW!

3. Include long-term visions and desires as well as images of things you know are possible for you in the short term. Size doesn't matter to the Universe, but we manifest what we believe is possible for us as individuals. This is a great way to increase your faith in manifesting as a process, as you tick off all you receive.

4. Remembering to use affirmations for programming and positive self-talk can become easier if you put them on your board. Choose powerful statements, desired feelings, or words of intention that you wish to embody such as balance or strength.

5. Put your board somewhere visible and make it a rolling project. Ask yourself what energy you have channeled toward those desires recently. There is always an aligned action in the Law of Attraction.

WEEK 1 INTENTIONS:
YOUR ENERGY IS EVERYTHING

Since we manifest from the inside out, it's important to keep investing in ourselves energetically. We need to understand what adds to us, lifts us, nourishes us, and returns us to love. Think about the following this week:

★ HOW DO YOU WANT TO FEEL?

★ WHAT MAKES YOU FEEL LIKE YOU?

★ WHAT OR WHO RAISES YOUR VIBRATION OR MOVES YOUR ENERGETIC STATE?

★ WHAT ALIGNED ACTIONS WILL SUPPORT YOUR DESIRED FEELINGS AND ENERGY THIS WEEK?

SOUL FOOD FOR THOUGHT

Allow yourself time to nurture your energy, so that your practice is consistent, but fluid and filled with intuitive compassion. Create a list of things that restore your body, mind, and spirit, then choose daily what works for you. Be flexible with your needs.

WEEK 1 FOCUS:
ENERGY

**Use the three prompts each day to help
you think about your energy:**

Prompt 1 What are you grateful for that gives you energy today?

Prompt 2 What will nourish your body, mind, or spirit today?

Prompt 3 What energetic signal do you want to send out? Consider your aura:
"My aura is _____" (for example, magnetic/fun/confident!).

Monday

Tuesday

Wednesday

Thursday

_____

_____

_____

Friday

_____

_____

_____

Saturday

_____

_____

_____

Sunday

_____

_____

_____

"INTENTIONALLY CONSIDER WHERE YOUR ENERGY IS PLACED IN EACH MOMENT. WHAT YOU FOCUS ON NOW HAS THE POWER TO INFLUENCE WHAT COMES NEXT."

WEEK 1 REFLECTIONS

Your time and energy are precious, so focus on what is in your control—your vibration, your perception, and your actions and reactions. Look back over the last week and think about the following:

Name three blessings, big or small, from this week. How did they make you feel?

1. _____

2. _____

3. _____

What or who did you give most of your energy to this week?

_____

_____

How did you top up your energy cup this week—perhaps by resting, meditating, or spending time with friends?

_____

_____

Is there anything that consumed your energy, perhaps more than necessary?

_____

_____

Where would you like to focus your energy more going forward?

_____

_____

WEEK 2 INTENTIONS:
ATTITUDE OF GRATITUDE

Believe it or not, you have manifested so much already just by being you! So, imagine all the amazing things you'll start noticing by shifting your energy each day. Once we receive our manifestations, we shouldn't take them for granted; let's continue to send love to all you have already received, as what you focus on multiplies! Think about the following this week:

★ HOW DO YOU WANT TO FEEL?

★ WHAT OR WHO ARE FIVE BEAUTIFUL BLESSINGS YOU HAVE ALREADY RECEIVED IN YOUR LIFE?

★ HOW CAN YOU APPRECIATE YOURSELF MORE? CONSIDER HOW YOU SHOW YOUR APPRECIATION OF OTHERS, TOO.

★ WHAT ALIGNED ACTIONS WILL SUPPORT YOUR DESIRED FEELINGS AND HELP YOU SPREAD THE ENERGY OF GRATITUDE THIS WEEK?

SOUL FOOD FOR THOUGHT

It's more powerful to take time to connect with the feeling of true gratitude, rather than just whittling off a list of the same old things out of a fear you're going to miss out on your manifestations. Let your practices be driven by love, not fear.

WEEK 2 FOCUS:
GRATITUDE

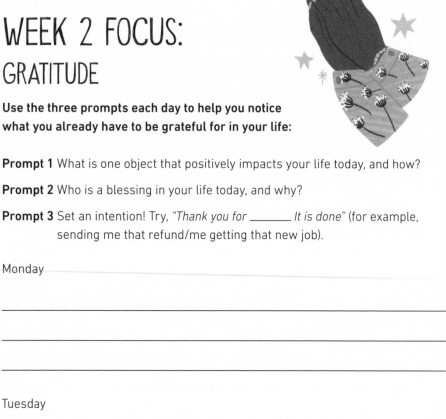

Use the three prompts each day to help you notice what you already have to be grateful for in your life:

Prompt 1 What is one object that positively impacts your life today, and how?

Prompt 2 Who is a blessing in your life today, and why?

Prompt 3 Set an intention! Try, *"Thank you for _____ It is done"* (for example, sending me that refund/me getting that new job).

Monday

_____

_____

_____

Tuesday

_____

_____

_____

Wednesday

_____

_____

_____

Thursday

_____

_____

_____

Friday

_____

_____

_____

Saturday

_____

_____

_____

Sunday

_____

_____

_____

"THE LAW OF ATTRACTION IS RESPONDING TO YOU,
SO DON'T WAIT FOR SOMETHING TO MANIFEST
BEFORE FINDING A REASON TO SMILE."

WEEK 2 REFLECTIONS

It's important to notice all the ways in which we are receiving. For instance, getting an unexpected free drink or money off a bill. Why not make a list on your phone every time you receive something—you'll be surprised how it all adds up! Look back over the last week and think about the following:

Name three blessings, big or small, from this week. How did they make you feel?

1. _____

2. _____

3. _____

What were your five favorite moments of the week, and why?

_____

_____

What one decision did you make last week that you are thankful for, and why?

_____

_____

How did you show gratitude this week?

_____

_____

How does feeling deep gratitude impact your day?

_____

_____

WEEK 3 INTENTIONS:
"I AM A MAGNET FOR MIRACLES!"

We manifest from a place of self-concept, which includes what we are being, how we feel about ourselves, and, ultimately, who we believe ourselves to be. And trust me, you're already awesome. It's time to start seeing yourself for the wonder that you are. Miracles are inevitable. Think about the following this week:

★ HOW DO YOU WANT TO FEEL?

★ WHAT MAKES YOU AN AWESOME PERSON?

★ WHAT ARE YOU REALLY GOOD AT?

★ WHAT ALIGNED ACTIONS WILL SUPPORT YOUR DESIRED FEELINGS AND HELP YOU NOTICE WHAT A WONDERFUL HUMAN BEING YOU ARE?

SOUL FOOD FOR THOUGHT

You do you. We get told who to be, what to wear, what will make us likeable and loveable, and so on. This is your story to write and you are the main character. This journey is your chance to tap into the authentic you with your own unique shine!

WEEK 3 FOCUS:
SELF-CONCEPT

Use the three prompts each day to help you value and appreciate your authentic self. You have so many reasons to value the wonder of you:

Prompt 1 How are you making yourself proud? Note down, *"I am proud of the way I _____"* (for example, make my bed each morning/care for friends).

Prompt 2 How do you bring value to the world?

Prompt 3 Affirm with me: *"I am totally _____"* (for example, awesome/worthy).

Monday

_____

_____

_____

Tuesday

_____

_____

_____

Wednesday

_____

_____

_____

Thursday

_____

_____

_____

Friday

_____

_____

_____

Saturday

_____

_____

_____

Sunday

_____

_____

_____

**"YOU'RE DOING YOUR BEST AND DESERVE TO BE BLESSED.
YOU DON'T HAVE TO PASS THROUGH A STORM ALONE BEFORE
THE UNIVERSE WILL THROW YOU A LIFELINE."**

WEEK 3 REFLECTIONS

You can come into a place of acceptance for all you are now, while still holding a vision for all that you're blossoming into. You are a perfect work in progress. Look back over the last week and think about the following:

Name three blessings, big or small, from this week. How did they make you feel?

1. _____

2. _____

3. _____

What did you do well this week?

_____

_____

How were you a blessing to others?

_____

_____

What praise would you like to give yourself right now?

_____

_____

How can you be kinder to yourself going forward?

_____

_____

WEEK 4 INTENTIONS:
YOU'RE ALREADY A SUCCESS

Success is an inside job. We can get caught up in the narrative of "I'll be a success when...", but this just holds us in the vibration of lack and feeling incomplete. The key is to see how you're already a success and to create a feeling of success on your own terms. Think about the following this week:

★ HOW DO YOU WANT TO FEEL?

★ WHAT DOES SUCCESS MEAN TO YOU?

★ WHAT ACTIVITIES, NO MATTER HOW SMALL, GIVE YOU A FEELING OF SATISFACTION?

★ WHAT ALIGNED ACTIONS WILL SUPPORT YOUR DESIRED FEELINGS AND HELP YOU NOTICE HOW YOU'RE ALREADY WINNING AT LIFE THIS WEEK?

SOUL FOOD FOR THOUGHT

Take the pressure off yourself that every day must look like high-speed momentum and big wins. It's not always awards season for an Oscar-winning actor! There is power in your rest and you're enough in the stillness.

WEEK 4 FOCUS:
SUCCESS MINDSET

Use the three prompts each day to help you celebrate "you" just as you are, as well as what you have already achieved in your life.

Prompt 1 Remember a time of success, then connect to the feeling you had:
"I felt so successful when I _____" (for example, decluttered my space)

Prompt 2 How are you already good enough?

Prompt 3 What can you achieve today that will make you feel proud of yourself? Remember, the to-do list is never done. Aim for balance over burnout.

Monday

_____

_____

_____

Tuesday

_____

_____

_____

Wednesday

_____

_____

_____

Thursday

_____

_____

_____

Friday

_____

_____

_____

Saturday

_____

_____

_____

Sunday

_____

_____

_____

"THE LAW OF ATTRACTION REQUIRES YOU TO BECOME A VIBRATIONAL MATCH TO WHAT YOU DESIRE. BE YOUR OWN CHEERLEADER AND EMBODY THE ENERGY OF SUCCESS FIRST."

WEEK 4 REFLECTIONS

Keep taking the pressure off yourself. Focus less on how far you have to go and more on how far you have already come. Remember your power! Look back over the last week and think about the following:

Name three blessings, big or small, from this week. How did they make you feel?

1. _____

2. _____

3. _____

What did you achieve this week?

_____

_____

How can you reward or celebrate yourself?

_____

_____

How can you enjoy the journey and not just the destination?

_____

_____

How can you notice your successes daily going forward?

_____

_____

SUCCESS STORY
ESTHER

What could be more powerful than telling you that this book was on my intentions list!?

In September 2021, on a guided meditation journey meeting my future self, I asked her for the next steps I should take to publish a book. She held up a red string full of stickie notes and said: "You already have everything you need to write your book here."

After downloading an image of a book for my vision board and one unfruitful pitch (which was me energetically throwing my hat in the ring), my publishers reached out. Here we are, one year later, lovingly creating this book for you.

Spirit is your sat nav and it knows the quickest route to your destination.

TRUST THE PROCESS...

Embodying spiritual practices might feel like a lot of rules, but don't create another hamster wheel for yourself when you've been trying to get off the one society gave you. You have permission to do this your way!

Reminder: Keep referring back to your Vision Board to reaffirm all that you wish to manifest. Hold on to your dreams!

CYCLE 2:
CONNECT TO THE STREAM

In our second cycle together, we are focusing on connecting to the stream of love, abundance, and flow that is available to us all, if we allow it energetically. The more we trust, the more we focus on what we are being, and the more we prioritize what brings us joy, the more we allow our personal path to happiness to arise. However, so many of us are collectively conditioned to the "all work and very little play" hustle culture, which leaves us feeling burned out, bitter, and disconnected from pleasure. Disclaimer alert: it can feel uncomfortable to release control by prioritizing play and flow over traditional working efforts because this may feel counterintuitive, lazy, or even risky. So, don't worry if these feelings arise; we're going to take things gently.

Time to dive in, or at the very least, dip a toe in the flow.

INTENTION-SETTING EXERCISE:
3 X 33 METHOD

It's a numbers game. One of the keys to effective subconscious programming is repetition, and this technique works on the basis that you're repeating an affirmation. Hopefully, you'll find this a simple and effective technique. It is great for trying out "small" manifestations and when you're building your belief in the manifesting process. You may also have seen this technique done as the 5 x 55 method, which is identical, but just includes more affirmations over more days. Do what feels right for you here.

1. Choose an affirmation stating that your manifestation has been received and write it on the line below. Try: "Thank you for my _____ It is done." Writing in the past or present tense affirms that the wish has already been fulfilled.

   _____

2. Repeat your affirmation 33 times for three days. You can write it down, record a voice note on your phone, say it out loud in the shower—anything goes! Choose what feels fun to you for this exercise because you want to enjoy the process. Try to connect to the belief that it is really done and how wonderful this feels—be the energy you want to attract.

3. If you miss a day or miscount the affirmations slightly, that's fine, as you can just pick up where you left off. Remember, it's more about your belief and feeling connected to your manifesting power. The magic wand is only as powerful as the magician who wields it.

4. If you feel that you have gone wrong, you have permission to start again—this may soothe you energetically. But remember, once it's done, it's done! The Universe got your order. Time to detach and get off topic, which this cycle should help you with.

WEEK 5 INTENTIONS:
FUN TIMES AHEAD

Manifestation really isn't meant to be all serious. You have full permission to be light and playful because, energetically, that's where the magic happens. Fun shouldn't just be a reward at the end of a 9–5 week, but an energetic thread that runs through your day. Think about the following this week:

★ HOW DO YOU WANT TO FEEL?

★ WHAT DID YOU LIKE TO DO FOR FUN AS A CHILD?

★ WHAT DO YOU USUALLY DO FOR FUN IN THE PRESENT?

★ WHAT ALIGNED ACTIONS WILL SUPPORT YOUR DESIRED FEELINGS AND HELP YOU ENJOY FUN TIMES THIS WEEK?

SOUL FOOD FOR THOUGHT

The manifesting cycle is like a relay race. There's a time for aligned action, which is when you run your lap. But when you run out of actions to take, your lap has ended. Rather than coming up with thousands of ideas to force progress, this is your time to hand over the baton to the Universe and to rest and recharge. With your focus being on fun and trusting in the process, you allow the Universe to run its lap, lining up the components until it is your turn to take up the baton again.

WEEK 5 FOCUS:
FUN

Use the three prompts each day to help you see where you can just relax, have fun, and enjoy the life you already have:

Prompt 1 What feels like fun for you today?

Prompt 2 What feels like a nice way to end your day?

Prompt 3 What activities can you be truly present for that have nothing to do with your manifestation?

Monday

_____

_____

_____

Tuesday

_____

_____

_____

Wednesday

_____

_____

_____

Thursday

_____

_____

_____

Friday

_____

_____

_____

Saturday

_____

_____

_____

Sunday

_____

_____

_____

**" YOU'RE ALLOWED TO
LOVE YOUR LIFE NOW AND STILL
DREAM OF MORE. "**

WEEK 5 REFLECTIONS

Fun is a fantastic tool for getting off topic and helping you to detach from your manifestations. The needier we feel about a manifestation, the more it continues to elude us. Fun is your superpower. Look back over the last week and think about the following:

Name three blessings, big or small, from this week. How did they make you feel?

1. _____

2. _____

3. _____

What were your top five fun moments of the week, and why?

_____

_____

What does fun, play, and pleasure bring to your life?

_____

_____

Did anything drain your energy, which you would like to be more aware of?

_____

_____

How would you like to prioritize fun more going forward?

_____

_____

WEEK 6 INTENTIONS:
GIVE A LITTLE LOVE

You are divine love in human form and, in my experience, when your manifestations are supercharged with caring intentions that create a wider impact, they become energetically supercharged. Whoosh! Think about the following this week:

★ HOW DO YOU WANT TO FEEL?

★ CONSIDER SOME OF YOUR MANIFESTATIONS—HOW COULD RECEIVING THEM POSITIVELY IMPACT SOMEONE ELSE IN YOUR SPHERE OF INFLUENCE?

★ HOW DOES IT MAKE YOU FEEL SEEING THOSE YOU LOVE BEING BLESSED?

★ WHAT ALIGNED ACTIONS WILL SUPPORT YOUR DESIRED FEELINGS AND HELP YOU SPREAD THE ENERGY OF LOVE THIS WEEK?

SOUL FOOD FOR THOUGHT

When we feel that we lack something, it can be challenging to see someone else get what we are asking for. But jealousy only holds us in this vibration by reinforcing that we haven't achieved our manifestation yet. When you see someone with something you want, celebrate with them; their win is not only a sign that it's showing up in your energy field, but it also represents an opportunity to allow it in by showing it the right kind of attention.

WEEK 6 FOCUS:
LOVE

Use the three prompts each day to help you spread love and show your appreciation of other people this week:

Prompt 1 If you could tell someone you love them today, who would it be?

Prompt 2 Bring awareness into your day—how can you leave other people feeling better than when you found them?

Prompt 3 Manifest for someone else! Perhaps, *"Thank you for _____ receiving _____. It is done"* (for example, Josh receiving a new job).

Monday

_____

_____

_____

Tuesday

_____

_____

_____

Wednesday

_____

_____

_____

hursday

_____

_____

_____

riday

_____

_____

_____

Saturday

_____

_____

_____

Sunday

_____

_____

_____

"THE FORCE IS ALWAYS WITHIN YOU BECAUSE SOURCE IS ALWAYS WITHIN YOU."

WEEK 6 REFLECTIONS

If you give a little love, it all comes back to you. If you give to someone and they are unable to return that energy, that's okay. When you give from your heart, it will all come back round from some other source; it isn't a tit-for-tat exchange. Look back over the last week and think about the following:

Name three blessings, big or small, from this week. How did they make you feel?

1. _____

2. _____

3. _____

How did you love others this week?

_____

_____

How does it make you feel to spread love throughout your day?

_____

_____

Treat others how you would like to be treated. How do you like to be treated?

_____

_____

How can you give love on a larger scale? Remember, this world needs your magic.

_____

_____

WEEK 7 INTENTIONS: EVERYTHING IN ABUNDANCE

Abundance is an infinite and overflowing stream of blessings that we can all access, and not just synonymous with material wealth. From an abundance of eligible partners to career options and leaves on a tree, there is enough for everyone and always an option for you. Think about the following this week:

★ HOW DO YOU WANT TO FEEL?

★ WHAT DOES ABUNDANCE MEAN TO YOU PERSONALLY?

★ WHERE DO YOU ALREADY ENJOY ABUNDANCE IN YOUR LIFE?

★ WHAT ALIGNED ACTIONS WILL SUPPORT YOUR DESIRED FEELINGS AND HELP YOU CONNECT TO THE ENERGY OF ABUNDANCE THIS WEEK?

SOUL FOOD FOR THOUGHT

Be aware of the current social narratives going around that may make you feel cut off from abundance and possibilities. Narratives such as "Nobody is spending money right now" or "There are no good people on dating apps" don't have to be a truth you accept personally. Create your own truths and look for evidence that supports your narrative.

WEEK 7 FOCUS:
ABUNDANCE

Use the three prompts each day to help you recognize how much abundance you already have in your life. Remember, abundance is here for you now:

Prompt 1 Affirm with me: *"I have an abundance of _____ that makes me feel _____*

Prompt 2 A manifestation can come to you in so many ways. Describe briefly how your manifestation could be received. What could happen for you?

Prompt 3 Choose one room in your home: work out the financial worth or value the contents bring to your life. Abundance is here for you now.

Monday

_____

_____

_____

Tuesday

_____

_____

_____

Wednesday

_____

_____

_____

hursday

_____

_____

_____

riday

_____

_____

_____

aturday

_____

_____

_____

unday

_____

_____

_____

**"IF YOU EVER FIND YOURSELF WORRYING WHERE YOUR
BLESSINGS ARE, NEVER UNDERESTIMATE THE UNIVERSE'S LOVE
FOR YOU AND ITS POWER TO MOVE MOUNTAINS."**

WEEK 7 REFLECTIONS

You deserve abundance. We create and allow what we believe is possible for us. In time, nurturing your self-worth will be the abundance-manifesting ace up your sleeve. Look back over the last week and think about the following:

Name three blessings, big or small, from this week. How did they make you feel?

1. _____

2. _____

3. _____

What made you feel abundant this week?

_____

_____

In what ways do you feel content right now?

_____

_____

What makes you deserving of more abundance? Remember, there is no limit to being blessed.

_____

_____

Who can you spend time with from now on who dreams big and thinks expansively?

_____

_____

WEEK 8 INTENTIONS:
LESS IS MORE

As well as being fun to do, manifesting is also not supposed to be hard. It's a cyclical balancing act between taking inspired action and knowing when to step away, trusting that the Universe will present the next stepping stone. Think about the following this week:

★ HOW DO YOU WANT TO FEEL?

★ WHAT CAN YOU TAKE OFF YOUR TO-DO LIST THIS WEEK? IN OTHER WORDS, WHAT CAN TRULY WAIT OR MIGHT BE UNNECESSARY RIGHT NOW?

★ IN WHAT WAYS DO YOU NORMALLY PUSH OR OBSESS? PERHAPS YOU KEEP CHECKING FOR EMAILS OR WHETHER YOU'VE MADE A SALE.

★ WHAT ALIGNED ACTIONS WILL SUPPORT YOUR DESIRED FEELINGS AND HELP YOU PUSH LESS AND REST MORE?

SOUL FOOD FOR THOUGHT

What looks like one person's path to success may not be the right fit for you. It's all too easy to sign up to a blueprint of "I must do X to receive or achieve this," but your desires can be received in your own unique way. Often, an inspired idea will hit you like a lightening bolt—follow that nudge, it's for you!

WEEK 8 FOCUS:
DO LESS

Use the three prompts each day to help you work out how you can receive what you want more easily:

Prompt 1 What feels like a "get to" action instead of "should do" action today?

Prompt 2 What could slowing down or resting look like for you today?

Prompt 3 Can you remember a time when you received something effortlessly? Remember: it wasn't too good to be true, as this can be your normal reality, full of ease and surprises!

Monday

_____

_____

_____

Tuesday

_____

_____

_____

Wednesday

_____

_____

_____

Thursday

_____

_____

_____

Friday

_____

_____

_____

Saturday

_____

_____

_____

Sunday

_____

_____

_____

"YOUR MANIFESTATION REQUIRES FAITH IN THE UNSEEN FORCE OF LOVE THAT FLOWS THROUGH EACH AND EVERY ONE OF US. IT'S NOT ALL ON YOU."

WEEK 8 REFLECTIONS

You aren't a robot. If we could slow down and detach on a whim, we'd be instant manifestation masters! Be patient with yourself as you take your foot off the gas when required. Look back over the last week and think about the following

Name three blessings, big or small, from this week. How did they make you feel?

1. _____

2. _____

3. _____

How did you push less or slow down this week?

_____

_____

How has prioritizing rest supported your spirit this week?

_____

_____

What's already going well for you right now?

_____

_____

How can you be more aware of where you might be pushing and energetically sabotaging the process?

_____

_____

SUCCESS STORY
LAURA

Laura had launched a new offer in her business and wanted to call in, ideally, three new clients. But she had not even found one at the new price she was charging and felt she would be grateful just to see that first sign-up.

Using the *3 x 33 Method* (see page 38), she recorded: "Thank you for my new client" in her voice phone notes for three days.

Not only did Laura get her first sign-up, but she got all three! Feeling more empowered, she then decided to set the intention again, but this time asking for another three clients. It worked and in total she got six new clients within the month.

Don't be surprised when the Universe overdelivers on what you asked for when you connect to the abundant stream.

TRUST THE PROCESS...

Every time you desire a new manifestation, it can bring new attachments, so be gentle with yourself, as you may need to relearn how to let your manifestations unfold. You will most likely find yourself revisiting how to embody trust, but your ability to detach and flow will get stronger each time. Stay the course!

I AM AN
UNSTOPPABLE,
POWERFUL,
CREATIVE
FORCE OF NATURE.

CYCLE 3:
BACK DOWN TO EARTH

In our third cycle together, we are going to spend some time being present in the physical realm and nurturing aspects of our 3D reality. We are nature itself and connecting with its forces can help us to remember our divine essence and sovereignty as spiritual guardians of this beautifully abundant planet. Also, focusing on nurturing what you have created in the 3D world, including your money or possessions, does not make you materialistic. We are here to work energetically in the higher dimensions to create and then experience bliss in our human 3D form. Everything in our lives is spiritual; there is room for it all.

Let's return to our roots.

TECHNIQUE TO TRY:
SCRIPTING

The person we think we are is often a character, programmed with a backstory and set of beliefs that are handed to us. As you embark on your spiritual journey know that your limitless true essence lies beneath it all. Scripting allows you t create a new story, even a new character. It's your story to write and, remember there is no failure in choosing a new path when the old one no longer aligns.

1. Grab a piece of paper and write: "Thank you, thank you, thank you for receiving [insert your manifestation] that serves me for my highest and greatest good, and for the highest and greatest good of the collective."

2. Focus on the area of your life in which you're manifesting change. State what you're already grateful for in this area because this allows you to approach the topic from a place of acceptance and abundance. You could use a statement such as: "I fully love, see, and accept [chosen life area] as you are."

3. Then describe your manifestation in detail as if it's already been received. Include how it unfolded with ease and the reasons why you love it. It could be as simple as "It looks beautiful" or "It gives me freedom." What you want will largely be aligned with your personal values.

4. Move on to describing how your manifestation will impact your life and anybody else's going forward. Plus, how will you show up differently as a result? Connect to the future you!

5. From the concept of "living in the end," write down how you'll feel when this is all done. Connect to gratitude from that end place. An extra tip here: ask yourself where you're already feeling this in your life, so you can seal it off with the energy of contentment. Finish the script with the following words: "And so it is, abracadabra, or amen," or any phrase that resonates with you.

6. When you're done, pop the written manifestation somewhere safe; perhaps under a plant pot or in a special box for your intention scripts.

WEEK 9 INTENTIONS:
GROUND YOURSELF

A feeling we all seek that is intrinsic to happiness and contentment is to find a place of inner safety and stability. In grounding or "earthing" ourselves, we can come home to our body, find presence, and reconnect to the earth, as well as enjoy other health benefits. Think about the following this week:

★ HOW DO YOU WANT TO FEEL?

★ HOW WOULD YOU DEFINE "GROUNDING" FOR YOURSELF PERSONALLY?

★ WHAT ACTIVITIES GIVE YOU DEEP CONTENTMENT OR SOOTHE YOUR SOUL?

★ WHAT ALIGNED ACTIONS WILL SUPPORT YOUR DESIRED FEELINGS AND HELP YOU GROUND YOUR ENERGY?

SOUL FOOD FOR THOUGHT

Some of the best ways to ground include walking barefoot on grass or sand, lying down on the ground, swimming or just paddling in a stream, and practicing deep breathwork out in nature. What sounds soothing for you?

WEEK 9 FOCUS:
GROUNDING

Use the three prompts each day to help ground your spirit and earth bodies, and allow yourself to find a place of safety and contentment:

Prompt 1 What is one thing you appreciate about nature today, and why?

Prompt 2 How could you connect with Mother Nature today? Think of the elements: earth, air, water, and fire if you need inspiration.

Prompt 3 Is there anything you need to let go of or prioritize today in order to nurture your inner peace?

Monday

Tuesday

Wednesday

Thursday

_____

_____

_____

Friday

_____

_____

_____

Saturday

_____

_____

_____

Sunday

_____

_____

_____

**"IF OUR ATTENTION
IS THE WATER, WE CAN
CHOOSE TO GROW EITHER
WEEDS OR FLOWERS."**

WEEK 9 REFLECTIONS

Mother Nature is sacred. As we reconnect to her wisdom and healing through grounding, ask yourself how you can give back to her and cherish her gifts more, as an energy exchange. Look back over the last week and think about the following:

Name three blessings, big or small, from this week. How did they make you feel?

1. _____

2. _____

3. _____

How did you connect with nature this week?

_____

_____

What soothed your soul the most, and why?

_____

_____

What season of your life are you now in and what are you transforming into?

_____

_____

Where can you start giving back to the planet through conscious choices?

_____

_____

WEEK 10 INTENTIONS:
NO TIME LIKE THE PRESENT

Your future is manifesting from a series of "now" moments, so your power to create change with your intention lies in the present moment. What would you like to give your energy and focus to? Think about the following this week:

★ HOW DO YOU WANT TO FEEL?

★ WHAT DOES BEING TRULY PRESENT LOOK LIKE FOR YOU?

★ WHAT WOULD YOUR FUTURE SELF BE FOCUSING ON (PERHAPS UPGRADING YOUR WARDROBE, GROWING A BUSINESS, OR INVESTING MONEY)? SHOW UP AS THEM!

★ WHAT ALIGNED ACTIONS WILL SUPPORT YOUR DESIRED FEELINGS AND HELP YOU TO BE PRESENT THIS WEEK?

SOUL FOOD FOR THOUGHT

When we are truly present, time feels as if it's flying. In that energetic space there is no resistance; we are just being with whatever we are doing. No preoccupied thoughts or concerns, just being here, right now. What activities make time fly for you?

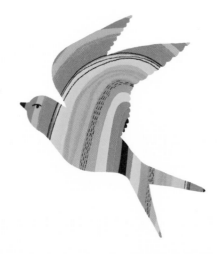

WEEK 10 FOCUS:
PRESENCE

Use the three prompts each day to help you utilize the power of the present moment. Being present today will reap rewards in the future:

Prompt 1 What would you like to be present with today? This looks like giving something your full attention, with all your senses and no distractions.

Prompt 2 What thoughts would you like to choose today?

Prompt 3 How will these choices serve you, support you, help you to grow, or nourish you?

Monday

Tuesday

Wednesday

hursday

_____

_____

_____

riday

_____

_____

_____

Saturday

_____

_____

_____

Sunday

_____

_____

_____

"LIVING TODAY CREATES MY TOMORROW;
LOVING MYSELF ALLOWS ME TO BLOSSOM AND
WHAT I BELIEVE IS WHAT I'LL PERCEIVE."

WEEK 10 REFLECTIONS

When you are self-aware and present with what you are being or doing, you can break patterns of limitation and find higher ways of operating. Look back over the last week and think about the following:

Name three blessings, big or small, from this week. How did they make you feel?

1. _____

2. _____

3. _____

What were you present or intentional with this week?

_____

_____

What helps ground you and brings you into the now?

_____

_____

What do you notice when truly present—perhaps in your surroundings or body?

_____

_____

Is there anything that deserves more presence in your life? What could a first step in this direction look like?

_____

_____

WEEK 11 INTENTIONS: MONEY

Money is just an energetic tool that you can wield to create impact in your life and for the wider collective. As such, you are the master of your money. It's time to take your power back and turn money into a friend who wants to help and support you. Think about the following this week:

★ HOW DO YOU WANT TO FEEL?

★ WHAT IS POSSIBLE FOR YOU FINANCIALLY AND WHERE COULD MONEY COME FROM?

★ HOW DOES RECEIVING MONEY SUPPORT YOUR OWN INTENTIONS?

★ WHAT ALIGNED ACTIONS WILL SUPPORT YOUR DESIRED FEELINGS AND HELP YOU NURTURE YOUR MONEY THIS WEEK?

SOUL FOOD FOR THOUGHT

Respect your cash flow and put out a signal that you're ready for more. To do this, check your bank account regularly, set up a penny jar (so you have money energy around you), clear out your purse or wallet to make space for new money to flow into, and, of course, have a budget! These ideas may seem obvious but, energetically, avoiding looking at your money only separates us further from calling in more.

WEEK 11 FOCUS:
YOUR FINANCES

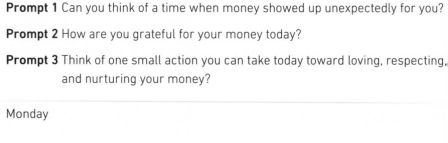

**Use the three prompts each day to help
you nuture your relationship with money.
Remember, give money the attention that it deserves:**

Prompt 1 Can you think of a time when money showed up unexpectedly for you?

Prompt 2 How are you grateful for your money today?

Prompt 3 Think of one small action you can take today toward loving, respecting, and nurturing your money?

Monday

_____

_____

_____

Tuesday

_____

_____

_____

Wednesday

_____

_____

_____

Thursday

_____

_____

_____

Friday

_____

_____

_____

Saturday

_____

_____

_____

Sunday

_____

_____

_____

"INCOME ISN'T JUST ABOUT MONEY. IT'S ALSO THE FLOW OF ALL BLESSINGS INTO YOUR LIFE. ALIGN YOURSELF TO THE ENERGY OF ABUNDANCE BY SEEING ALL THAT'S INCOMING."

WEEK 11 REFLECTIONS

Keep reframing your relationship with money. It needs you to invest it, spend i **and love with it, so call it forward with your energy, love, and acceptance. Be a** **money magnet! Look back over the last week and think about the following:**

Name three blessings, big or small, from this week. How did they make you feel?

1. _____

2. _____

3. _____

How did you care for your money this week?

_____

_____

What were the last five bills you were able to pay? How do those bills support you and how do those payments potentially help the people you paid?

_____

_____

What are five favorite things or experiences money has allowed you to have?

_____

_____

What makes money good and welcome in your life? Learn to love money.

_____

_____

WEEK 12 INTENTIONS:
BOSS IT!

As we spend a great deal of time in our jobs, it's important to align with something that is a good match for you and your needs. Many people leave careers if they aren't aligned with their values. Let's lean into finding your perfect fit for emotional fulfillment. Think about the following this week:

★ HOW DO YOU WANT TO FEEL?

★ WHEN YOU WERE A CHILD, WHAT DID YOU WANT TO BE WHEN YOU GREW UP?

★ WHAT EVIDENCE DO YOU HAVE THAT YOU CAN DO SOMETHING YOU LOVE FOR A LIVING?

★ WHAT ALIGNED ACTIONS WILL SUPPORT YOUR DESIRED FEELINGS AND HELP YOU BRING YOUR BEST ENERGY TO YOUR WORK?

SOUL FOOD FOR THOUGHT

Whether you're applying for a job, or in an existing role, you can easily move into the energy of "I need this job." But the truth is, they need you! You're both a gift and an opportunity for them. Flip the switch and connect to how you're an asset! What do you have to offer a company, your customers, or even the world? What's meant for you won't pass you by!

WEEK 12 FOCUS:
YOUR CAREER

Use the three prompts each day to help you connect to feelings of contentment and inspiration around your career:

Prompt 1 What do you moan about in your job or in old jobs? What would the opposite of this look like? Build a "perfect job" clarity picture this week.

Prompt 2 Ask a colleague what they think you're good at. You may be surprised!

Prompt 3 What is one thing you can appreciate about your existing career today, and why (for example, your colleagues/money/growth)?

Monday

Tuesday

Wednesday

Thursday

_____

_____

_____

Friday

_____

_____

_____

Saturday

_____

_____

_____

Sunday

_____

_____

_____

**"WE ARE NEVER STUCK UNLESS WE SAY WE ARE—
THERE'S ALWAYS AN ENERGETIC WAY FORWARD AVAILABLE.
BELIEVE IN THE UNSEEN DOORS."**

WEEK 12 REFLECTIONS

It's important to accept what your current work offers and all you can give in return to combat feelings of lack. Your energy can create shifts at work or open up new career paths. Look back over the last week and think about the following

Name three blessings, big or small, from this week. How did they make you feel?

1. _____

2. _____

3. _____

What was your favorite piece of feedback at work this week, and why?

_____

_____

What generates feelings of success at work—how can you replicate this in future

_____

_____

What topics interest, excite, and inspire you?

_____

_____

What could expand your options professionally? Perhaps it's gaining a new skill or qualification, or starting a social media account to share what you love to do?

_____

_____

SUCCESS STORY
HANNAH

To be specific or not to be specific? That is the question!

Hannah had spent a long time looking for love and was always wondering: when will it be my turn? One day, she used *Scripting* (see page 58) to identify her ideal partner and wrote down a list of all the qualities she was looking for in terms of looks and, of course, their qualities and values.

Not too long afterward, Hannah's Mr. Right showed up, ticking all the boxes she had written on her list, which she showed me with much elation.

I have heard many success stories about people manifesting specific romantic partners, even down to someone's cooking abilities. This may feel impossible or like aligning with a needle in a haystack (I assure you, what you want is out there!), but, whatever approach you choose, be specific about the way your manifestation will make you feel. Happiness is the ultimate goal.

TRUST THE PROCESS...

From the metamorphosis of a butterfly to the shedding of leaves, nature embraces its own deconstruction, with trust and faith that it is becoming something more. You too are nature, so trust your own seasons of change and all you continue to blossom into.

Try it: Use a picture of your manifestation as a phone or laptop screensaver. This acts like an extension of your Vision Board, by continuing to reinforce your subconscious programming.

THERE'S SOMETHING MAGICAL ABOUT ME. I AM STARDUST, SPEAKING BLISS INTO EXISTENCE.

CYCLE 4:
MESSAGE IN A BOTTLE

In our fourth cycle together, we are exploring our personal language, which is available to lovingly support us, because in continuing to bring awareness to all that we are being, we allow ourselves to keep adjusting our magnetic signal and spot where we might be in resistance. As well as truly hearing the words that leave our lips, we can also listen and become conscious of how the Universe is communicating with us— giving us reassurance and evidence of our alignment with everything around us. Remember, the people around you might be earth angels, sent with a message or offering the helping hand you so needed to have today.

Let's open our ears, eyes, hearts, and minds to new truths, higher behaviors, and ways of being loved.

INTENTION-SETTING EXERCISE:
TWO-CUP METHOD

In this exercise you are channeling loving energy and intention into water and drinking it, letting it become a part of your being. This is often used for quantum jumping or reality shifting when you want to shift quickly into a higher version of yourself or a higher timeline that's available to you.

1. Get two cups, one filled with water and one without. You can use any cups, or one basic-looking cup and one that's a bit fancier to represent your upleveling.

2. Take two pieces of paper. On the first piece of paper write down all you have manifested so far, your current reality, and what you're grateful for. On the second piece, write: "Thank you for _____" and then, similarly to scripting, a shorter, encapsulated version of what you're calling in and how it will make you feel.

3. Take your first piece of "current reality paper" and the cup with water in it. Hold the water and look at the paper. You can read what the paper says out loud, or in your mind, or simply meditate on where you're at and how far you've come, and make peace with this.

4. When you're ready, take your second "new reality" paper and the empty cup. Pour the first cup of water into the second. Now sit and meditate on, visualize, say, or read what you wrote on the new reality paper, really connecting with how amazing this feels in your heart. Take your time with this and when you're done, drink the water.

5. I like to rip up or burn the first piece of paper because that's old news now and I keep the second piece somewhere safe. Remember, seek the feeling, not the thing. So, if you didn't know "what" you wanted, you can just work with the vibrations or feelings that you want to match.

Note: Why not research Dr Emoto's experiments on making beautiful water by creating a positive environment and having positive thoughts and emotions.

WEEK 13 INTENTIONS:
PIVOT! PIVOT!

Pivoting lets us shift our vibration and take back our power, as we refocus our thoughts—useful when we feel sad or need to turn our point of attraction around. But first we should recognize how we're feeling, rather than pushing this down. There's a place for all emotions as they guide us back to happiness. Think about the following this week:

★ HOW DO YOU WANT TO FEEL?

★ IF YOU'RE SAD, WHAT USUALLY TURNS THAT FROWN UPSIDE DOWN?

★ WHEN YOU FEEL CHALLENGED, WHAT, WHERE, OR WHO HELPS YOU PROCESS YOUR FEELINGS AND MOVE ON? LEAN INTO A SAFE SPACE.

★ WHAT ALIGNED ACTIONS WILL SUPPORT YOUR DESIRED FEELINGS AND HELP YOU KEEP MOVING TOWARD YOUR HAPPY PLACE THIS WEEK?

SOUL FOOD FOR THOUGHT

Sometimes the lesson we need to find or reframe isn't obvious, and what we're going through just feels rubbish. At times like these, we must love ourselves even more by processing our emotions. Don't get sucked into the toxic positivity or inner blame game, as this only creates more resistance.

WEEK 13 FOCUS:
PIVOTING

**Use the three prompts each day to help you pivot and reframe your thoughts.
If this feels challenging, use the EFT tool on page 136 to help shift your energy:**

Prompt 1 What does choosing your vibration or inner peace look like today?

Prompt 2 Which thoughts would you like to give your energy to today?
So, *"I would like to focus my thoughts on _____"* (for example,
financial possibilities/things I am doing well/all the love in my life).

Prompt 3 Remember your power! Recall a challenge you've grown from, and how?

Monday

_____

_____

_____

Tuesday

_____

_____

_____

Wednesday

_____

_____

_____

Thursday

_____

_____

_____

Friday

_____

_____

_____

Saturday

_____

_____

_____

Sunday

_____

_____

_____

"DIFFICULT TIMES ARE JUST THREADS IN THE TAPESTRY OF YOUR LIFE. A BIGGER, MORE BEAUTIFUL PICTURE IS ALWAYS AVAILABLE FOR YOU. ZOOM OUT, REMEMBER YOUR POWER, AND WEAVE A NEW STORY."

WEEK 13 REFLECTIONS

When we let something matter, it has power in our reality. But if it doesn't matter, why allow it to consume so much of our energy—only give focus to what you wish to keep in your vision. Look back over the last week and think about the following:

Name three blessings, big or small, from this week. How did they make you feel?

1. _____

2. _____

3. _____

How did you honor your feelings this week?

_____

_____

What's one lesson or powerful reflection you had this week?

_____

_____

How did you choose your vibration or pivot? How does it feel to run your own day?

_____

_____

Instead of being too reactive to life's challenges, how can you give them less power?

_____

_____

WEEK 14 INTENTIONS: KNOW YOUR LINGO

The words we use are a powerful indicator of our thoughts, the vibrational signal we are emitting, and thus what we are attracting back into our lives. Begin to listen to yourself, as your language can indicate what you believe is possible and whether you are in resistance or aligned to your manifestations. Think about the following this week:

★ HOW DO YOU WANT TO FEEL?

★ WHEN SOMEONE ASKS HOW YOU'RE DOING OR WHAT YOU'VE BEEN UP TO, WHAT DO YOU USUALLY FOCUS ON?

★ WHAT GOALS AND DREAMS CAN YOU START TALKING ABOUT WITH OTHERS—AND NOT JUST IN YOUR JOURNAL? MAKE IT REAL!

★ WHAT ALIGNED ACTIONS WILL SUPPORT YOUR DESIRED FEELINGS AND HELP YOU SPEAK MORE POWERFULLY THIS WEEK?

SOUL FOOD FOR THOUGHT

You are safe to steer a conversation and to explain that talking about something is making you feel uncomfortable. As Moira Rose in the TV sitcom *Schitt's Creek* said, "Gossip is the Devil's Telephone, best to just hang up." Having boundaries is part of loving yourself and leading others toward love.

WEEK 14 FOCUS:
LANGUAGE

Use the three prompts each day to help you make conscious language choices both when you interact with others and when talking to yourself:

Prompt 1 If someone asks how you are, how will you answer today?

Prompt 2 What types of conversation would you like to start or focus on today?

Prompt 3 Do you wish to let go of any words or phrases that hold you in limitation Perhaps you tell yourself off or affirm a manifestation still isn't here?

Monday

Tuesday

Wednesday

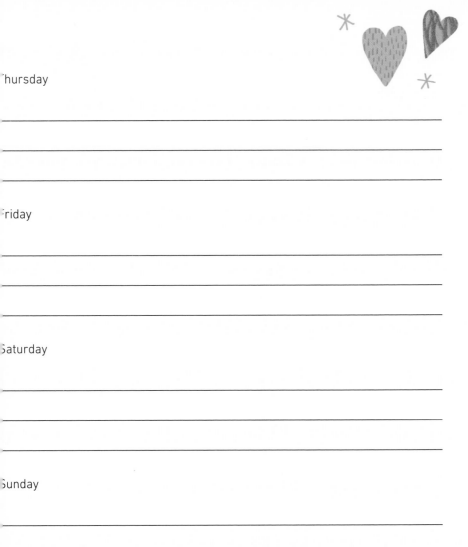

Thursday

_____

_____

_____

Friday

_____

_____

_____

Saturday

_____

_____

_____

Sunday

_____

_____

_____

"DECLARE YOUR GREATNESS, DECLARE YOUR ABUNDANCE,
DECLARE ALL YOUR BLESSINGS AND WHAT'S GOING WELL IN YOUR LIFE.
BE THE FREQUENCY OF CELEBRATION."

WEEK 14 REFLECTIONS

We aren't "trying" to manifest, as this implies a push and that it might not ever happen. Take out the "try" and affirm with me: "I *am* manifesting"!—there's no room for doubt here. Look back over the last week and think about the following

Name three blessings, big or small, from this week. How did they make you feel?

1. _____

2. _____

3. _____

What topics did you focus on in your conversations this week?

_____

_____

What's working out for you right now?

_____

_____

Did you make positive choices with your words or when steering conversations?

_____

_____

Are there any conversations that you'd like to cut out altogether because they are't serving your highest good? Do your words reveal areas of resistance to work on?

_____

_____

WEEK 15 INTENTIONS:
SIGNS AND SYNCHRONICITIES

There are no coincidences and whether you just put this down to everything being energetic or believe in higher guidance, we're always being guided and given evidence of our alignment through signs and synchronicities. Be on the look out for repeating numbers, unusual animals crossing your path, or songs you keep hearing. Think about the following this week:

★ HOW DO YOU WANT TO FEEL?

★ HAVE YOU EXPERIENCED SOMETHING "WEIRD" YOU PUT DOWN TO COINCIDENCE? OR ENJOYED A MOMENT OF RIGHT TIME, RIGHT PLACE?

★ HAVE YOU EVER THOUGHT ABOUT SOMEONE AND THEY SUDDENLY GOT IN TOUCH WITH YOU? WRITE ABOUT THIS IN A NOTEBOOK.

★ WHAT ALIGNED ACTIONS WILL SUPPORT YOUR DESIRED FEELINGS AND HELP YOU CONNECT TO THE UNIVERSE THIS WEEK?

SOUL FOOD FOR THOUGHT

We can sometimes get too hung up on what the signs mean. The Internet has a plethora of explanations, and usually the first thing you see will resonate, but if it doesn't, just let it be. Be thankful for the nudges, but don't get in a resistance spin worrying about what's going on—just stay self-aware. All will become clear.

WEEK 15 FOCUS:
GUIDANCE IS ALWAYS AVAILABLE

**Use the three prompts each day to help you nurture
your spiritual connection, remembering all that you have
learned so far about presence, grounding, and energetic focus:**

Prompt 1 What feels like the right thing to do today? Lean into your intuition and
needs. Guidance is available from within, not just from external sources

Prompt 2 What would make you feel spiritually connected today?

Prompt 3 What will serve your highest good today and keep you distracted and
detached from obsessing over receiving a sign?

Monday

_____

_____

_____

Tuesday

_____

_____

_____

Wednesday

_____

_____

_____

Thursday

Friday

Saturday

Sunday

"CALL ON THE UNIVERSE FOR A SIGN. ASK TO SEE ONE THING, MAYBE A ROBIN, LADYBUG, OR SNOWFLAKE. OR PICK TWO SYMBOLS AND SAY: SHOW ME THE WAY— A SUNFLOWER FOR THIS OR A HUMMINGBIRD FOR THAT."

WEEK 15 REFLECTIONS

Surround yourself with people who have also experienced signs and synchronicities. There is something so magical and validating when we hear other people's stories about how the divine is supporting their journeys too. You're not alone. Look back over the last week and think about the following:

Name three blessings, big or small, from this week. How did they make you feel?

1. _____

2. _____

3. _____

What made you feel most spiritually connected this week, and why?

_____

_____

What makes you feel loved and part of something bigger?

_____

_____

How does intuition feel in your body? Can you think of a time when it paid off?

_____

_____

How can you listen to your intuition and trust it more?

_____

_____

WEEK 16 INTENTIONS:
SHOWER COMPLIMENTS LIKE CONFETTI!

Receiving compliments is part of being in receiving mode. We can often be bashful, undermine ourselves, or downplay our awesomeness when someone points this out. You are amazing! Allow yourself to be in the energy of receiving love as well as giving it out. Think about the following this week:

★ HOW DO YOU WANT TO FEEL?

★ WHAT DO YOU LOVE TO BE COMPLIMENTED ON, AND WHY?

★ WHAT DO YOU NORMALLY SAY WHEN YOU RECEIVE A COMPLIMENT FROM SOMEONE? HOW CAN YOU BE MOST ACCEPTING OF IT?

★ WHAT ALIGNED ACTIONS WILL SUPPORT YOUR DESIRED FEELINGS AND HELP YOU GIVE OR ALLOW COMPLIMENTS THIS WEEK?

SOUL FOOD FOR THOUGHT

Ask yourself: "Where am I allowing myself to receive and where might I be blocking myself?" If someone offers to pay, let them. If someone offers to help, let them. Often, we don't want to be a bother or take up space and be a nuisance, but every time we say "No, don't worry about me, I'll be fine," we are denying the stream of support or abundance. You deserve to receive blessings in whatever form they take, guilt free! Allow it all.

WEEK 16 FOCUS:
ROMANCE YOURSELF

**Use the three prompts each day to help you connect with
your own self-worth, recognize your special gifts, and practice self-care:**

Prompt 1 What is one awesome thing about you today?

Prompt 2 Treat yourself in some way. Try, *"I would like to give myself the gift of
_____"* (for example, a bubble bath/quiet night in/massage).

Prompt 3 Affirm with me: *"I am truly worthy of _____"* (for example, abundance
reciprocal energy/self-care time).

Monday

_____

_____

_____

Tuesday

_____

_____

_____

Wednesday

_____

_____

_____

Thursday

_____

_____

_____

Friday

_____

_____

_____

Saturday

_____

_____

_____

Sunday

_____

_____

_____

"THERE IS A MAGIC INSIDE YOU THAT CAN BE A LIGHT IN DARK PLACES, AND SOMEONE WILL ALWAYS NEED YOUR SONG. YOU HAVE PERMISSION TO BELT OUT YOUR TRUTH."

WEEK 16 REFLECTIONS

Welcoming compliments doesn't make you big-headed. You deserve to feel love and celebrated, and that's what the compliment-giver wants. Allow yourself to shine brightly. Look back over the last week and think about the following:

Name three blessings, big or small, from this week. How did they make you feel?

1. _____

2. _____

3. _____

What was the nicest thing someone said to you this week?

_____

_____

What did you say when people complimented you or gave you positive feedback?

_____

_____

What did you compliment other people on, and why? Is that a reflection of what you value in yourself?

_____

_____

What love and light do you see in yourself right now?

_____

_____

SUCCESS STORY

STHER

ewind a few years. **After spending some time nconsciously manifesting big changes in my eality, I found myself in a patch of contrast nd frustration with my career. I was bored and nfulfilled. I knew I wanted to help people, but just didn't know how.**

fter many days trawling through job sites clutching t straws, but with no further clarity, I decided to do the *wo-Cup Method* (see page 78). I focused only on feelings s I had no other specifics I could work with, and let it go.

hortly after, I was doing a Law of Attraction course purely because I was iterested, and it mentioned coaching. Next, my workplace decided to launch a paching initiative in which I was able to take part. And then I saw a post for women's speaking summit that was accepting first-time speakers.

he rest is history. I put it out there and all the components aligned within a natter of three months. I am still feeling the effects of jumping into this timeline s I create this for you now. The key to success here was that I let it go, stopped 'ying to figure it all out, and focused on what was calling to me at that time.

TRUST THE PROCESS...

Sometimes we make more waves when we rock our own boats. Continue focusing on creating peace on the inside to create peace on the outside. Bring softness, compassion, and patience to your personal journey.

CYCLE 5:
TAKE THE HIGH WAY

In our fifth cycle together, we are continuing to nurture the concepts of flow, trust, and allowing. Manifestation is like baking. We create the ingredient mix through our energy and action, and then it goes into the oven. But we don't open the door to see if it's ready ahead of time as this can interfere with the process. Trust the oven and give your manifestation time to rise. While that divine cake is baking, we can lean into choosing ourselves, creative flow, and endless possibilities. We can often approach manifesting with tunnel-vision expectations of happiness, embodying that "it's my way or the highway" attitude. But our way is not always the High Way. Let's surrender the ego's ideas of what happiness means and allow ourselves to flow where Source carries us.

Buckle up, buttercup.

INTENTION-SETTING EXERCISE:
369 METHOD

The inventor Nikolai Tesla was fascinated by the number 369 and supposedly said it is a "key to the Universe." He would live aspects of his life by it, includir only staying in hotel rooms with a number divisible by three. Now don't panic— we're not about to start doing a Tesla and taking extra laps around the block. But we are going to harness the power of this number to manifest. There are many variations of this exercise, but I'm going to keep it as simple as possible

1. In the same way you did for the *3 x 33 Method* (see page 38), think of a simpl intention statement as if you have already received it and write it on the line below. For example: "I am so grateful for my _____. I feel so _____."

    _____

2. Now for three days in a row, you are going to say this statement out loud (you can also write or type it) at the following times:

    • **3pm**—say your statement three times

    • **6pm**—say your statement six times

    • **9pm**—say your statement nine times

    If these times don't work for you, just pick times of the day that do—I recommend setting an alarm for each time, so you don't forget.

3. As with all the previous exercises, the same basic rules apply:

    • The statement can be used for one or several manifestations. Pick what feels most believable and build up from there.

    • Connect to the feeling.

    • Do what feels good.

    • If you feel you have messed it up, repeat. Otherwise, once was enough.

4. And that's a wrap. Let it go and know it's on the way!

WEEK 17 INTENTIONS:
JUST SAY YES!

We can be so uncomfortable saying "no," but for every "no" you will find an empowered "yes" on the other side of it. Manifesting happiness comes down to you saying "yes" to your heart, "yes" to your dreams, "yes" to your genuine needs—it's time to say "yes" to yourself. Think about the following this week:

★ HOW DO YOU WANT TO FEEL?

★ WHAT DO YOU FIND IT DIFFICULT TO SAY "NO" TO, AND WHY?

★ IF YOU DO SAY "NO," WHAT EMPOWERED "YES" IS ON THE OTHER SIDE OF IT?

★ WHAT ALIGNED ACTIONS WILL SUPPORT YOUR DESIRED FEELINGS AND WHAT WOULD YOU LIKE TO SAY "YES" TO THIS WEEK?

SOUL FOOD FOR THOUGHT

As long as we speak and act out of love, we're not responsible for how others perceive us. We also shouldn't sacrifice our values or peace of mind to make other people feel comfortable. It's far better to like yourself than to dislike who you become when you compromise your truth to suit others.

WEEK 17 FOCUS:
SAY YES!

Use the three prompts each day to empower you to care about your feelings and connect to why choosing yourself is important for your expansion. Listen to what your heart truly wants and start finding ways to honor this:

Prompt 1 What do you get to say "yes" to today?

Prompt 2 How does honoring yourself support your expansion or desired feelings

Prompt 3 Allow yourself! Try, *"I have permission to say 'yes' to this because* _____
(for example, it helps me move on/I deserve better/it makes me happy

Monday

_____

_____

_____

Tuesday

_____

_____

_____

Wednesday

_____

_____

_____

Thursday

_____

_____

_____

Friday

_____

_____

_____

Saturday

_____

_____

_____

Sunday

_____

_____

_____

"BE FLEXIBLE WITH YOUR NEEDS. IT'S NOT ABOUT DOING THE SAME DAILY TASKS, BUT TRUSTING YOU'LL ALWAYS CHOOSE THE BEST LOVING RESPONSE TO YOUR EMOTIONS."

WEEK 17 REFLECTIONS

Boundaries indicate self-worth—they're self-respect in action! Give where you can, when you're able to and when it feels good, but know that if your energy cup is depleted or your intuition says "no," your obligation is to yourself. You're safe and can choose you. Look back over the last week and think about the following:

Name three blessings, big or small, from this week. How did they make you feel?

1. _____

2. _____

3. _____

What did you say "no" to this week?

_____

_____

What did you say "yes" to this week?

_____

_____

In what ways do you feel empowered?

_____

_____

Are your own actions serving you well? If not, what could you replace them with?

_____

_____

WEEK 18 INTENTIONS:
CREATIVE STREAK

Manifestation is pure creativity energy, as something
comes into being through you. In the same way as presence (see page 63),
when we are in a creative flow, there is no resistance and only the energy of
manifestation. You may not consider yourself creative, but problem-solving,
computer programming, gardening, cooking, and more all fall into this area.
What sparks your interest? Think about the following this week:

★ HOW DO YOU WANT TO FEEL?

★ HOW WOULD YOU CONSIDER YOURSELF TO BE CREATIVE?
CONSIDER WHAT YOU LIKED DOING AS A CHILD.

★ IS THERE ANYTHING NEW YOU'RE CURIOUS TO TRY,
WITHOUT JUDGMENT OR EXPECTATION? JUST FOR FUN!

★ WHAT ALIGNED ACTIONS WILL SUPPORT YOUR DESIRED FEELINGS
AND HELP YOU TAP INTO YOUR CREATIVE POWER THIS WEEK?

SOUL FOOD FOR THOUGHT

We often avoid creating something in case it is imperfect or perhaps not as good
as someone else's. Remember, everybody has a Chapter 1. You don't have to
create something to a standard; do it purely for the joy, love, presence, and
curiosity you experience from the process.

WEEK 18 FOCUS:
CREATIVITY

Use the three prompts each day to help you connect to your personal version of creativity and appreciate some of mankind's inventions. We are master creators and our imagination is a powerful gift:

Prompt 1 Look at all the inventions around you that were once just an idea. Choose one you greatly appreciate and write down why.

Prompt 2 Name something you enjoyed creating, whether as a child or recently.

Prompt 3 What could you create or how can you nurture your creativity today?

Monday

Tuesday

Wednesday

Thursday

_____

_____

_____

Friday

_____

_____

_____

Saturday

_____

_____

_____

Sunday

_____

_____

_____

"YOUR LIFE IS A CANVAS. YOUR ENERGY, THOUGHTS, ACTIONS, AND FEELINGS ARE PAINTS. BUT ULTIMATELY YOUR BELIEF IS THE BRUSH THAT BRINGS THE PAINTING TO LIFE."

WEEK 18 REFLECTIONS

Do what you love for passion over profit, but don't be surprised when profit naturally follows your passion. Profit can go where the energy flows. Look back over the last week and think about the following:

Name three blessings, big or small, from this week. How did they make you feel?

1. _____

2. _____

3. _____

How did you connect to creativity this week?

_____

_____

What is the kindest praise you can give yourself for what you've done or achieved this week?

_____

_____

What inspired or excited you the most this week?

_____

_____

How does making time to do something you enjoy serve you?

_____

_____

WEEK 19 INTENTIONS:
NORMALIZE SUCCESS

Have you ever noticed how easily some people seem to manifest money or find jobs or partners? It seems effortless for them. This is because somewhere in their self-concept (see page 27) there are beliefs that make this easy, if not normal. So, rather than putting your manifestations on a pedestal, start making them a normal part of your reality. Think about the following this week:

★ HOW DO YOU WANT TO FEEL?

★ WHAT DO YOU ASSUME IS FAIRLY DIFFICULT TO GET, MANIFEST, OR ACHIEVE?

★ WHAT IS THE EVIDENCE FOR THIS BEING TRUE? CHALLENGE YOURSELF AND LOOK AT SUCCESS STORIES TO THE CONTRARY TO SUPPORT HOW YOUR DESIRES COULD BE "NORMAL" FOR YOU.

★ WHAT ALIGNED ACTIONS WILL SUPPORT YOUR DESIRED FEELINGS AND HELP YOU TRUST THAT EASY SUCCESS IS POSSIBLE?

SOUL FOOD FOR THOUGHT

Continue to open yourself up to potential routes to success and fulfillment outside your expectations. Rather than limiting yourself when setting intentions, you can add this statement at the end: "This, or better, for the highest and greatest good of myself and the collective." Be open to magical surprises!

WEEK 19 FOCUS:
MIRACLES ARE NORMAL

Use the three prompts each day to help you connect to feelings of ease, infinit **possibilities, and that miracles can occur every day. Soon you'll barely have to** **think about what you want. It will flow into your life, naturally and consistently**

Prompt 1 What is possible for you today?

Prompt 2 Remember something that came easily to you—maybe a job or partne

Prompt 3 Affirm with me: *"Of course _____ come(s) naturally to me"* (for exampl
money/customers/opportunities).

Monday

Tuesday

Wednesday

Thursday

_____

_____

_____

Friday

_____

_____

_____

Saturday

_____

_____

_____

Sunday

_____

_____

_____

"WE CREATE WHAT WE BELIEVE IS POSSIBLE. LET GO OF YOUR LIMITS AND REMEMBER: YOU DESERVE ABUNDANCE. BELIEVE IN YOUR MAGIC, BELIEVE IN YOURSELF."

WEEK 19 REFLECTIONS

There's always an aligned action within the Law of Attraction, which may still involve "work" for you. But when it's right for you, it will bring all the happines you're seeking. There's a difference between burning out and burning brightly in your work. Look back over the last week and think about the following:

Name three blessings, big or small, from this week. How did they make you feel

1. _____

2. _____

3. _____

What felt like a success this week?

_____

_____

What do you now assume is easy to get, manifest, or achieve?

_____

_____

What is easy or comes naturally to you?

_____

_____

Why do your manifestations need you—for example, what gap do you fill for them

_____

_____

WEEK 20 INTENTIONS:
SWEET SURRENDER

Surrendering a manifestation doesn't mean you're giving up on it. But focusing so hard on a manifestation stops us enjoying the journey. So, hand over control of the timing, trust the work you have put in, and focus on how you feel, despite not seeing your manifestation materialize. Think about the following this week:

★ HOW DO YOU WANT TO FEEL?

★ TO EMBODY SURRENDER, WHAT ARE THE OPPOSITES OF PUSHING, FIGURING OUT THE FUTURE, OR TRYING TO FIX WHERE YOU ARE?

★ WHAT MAKES YOU FEEL TRUSTING OF THE PROCESS AND ABLE TO RELAX?

★ WHAT ALIGNED ACTIONS WILL SUPPORT YOUR DESIRED FEELINGS AND HELP YOU TRUST THE PROCESS?

SOUL FOOD FOR THOUGHT

Sometimes the best way to create momentum is to stop being a fixer. Have you noticed when the more you try to fix a problem, the more frustrated you get and nothing budges? So you give up. But when you come back, the solution just clicks. Manifesting is similar: step away from the issue energetically for a while, then return when you're in a better space.

WEEK 20 FOCUS:
TRUST

Use the three prompts each day to help you make peace with where you are on your journey. In dark times, there is always a light at the end of the tunnel:

Prompt 1 What do you feel content and satisfied with today?

Prompt 2 Recall a time when things seemed bleak, but everything worked out.

Prompt 3 Affirm with me: *"I trust the Universe and my unfolding path today because _____"* (for example, I'm surrounded by guidance/there are things still working out for me/every lesson has helped me become who I am).

Monday

_____

_____

_____

Tuesday

_____

_____

_____

Wednesday

_____

_____

_____

Thursday

_____

_____

_____

Friday

_____

_____

_____

Saturday

_____

_____

_____

Sunday

_____

_____

_____

"KNOWING YOU CAN TAKE YOUR EYES OFF THE
PRIZE BECAUSE IT'S ALWAYS WAITING AT
THE FINISH LINE, THAT'S REAL FAITH."

WEEK 20 REFLECTIONS

If you find yourself watching videos back-to-back on how to manifest something, then the chances are you're feeling needy and are trying to force the outcome. Step away from YouTube and bring it back to you. You are the magnet after all. Look back over the last week and think about the following:

Name three blessings, big or small, from this week. How did they make you feel?

1. _____

2. _____

3. _____

How did you surrender and detach this week?

_____

_____

In what ways can you go with the flow more and control the process less?

_____

_____

In what ways do you believe in yourself?

_____

_____

What does "bringing it back to you" mean for you going forward?

_____

_____

SUCCESS STORY
CAMERON

Cameron used the *369 Method* (see page 98) to receive a message from someone they hadn't heard from for a few months and didn't know if they were in good terms with anymore. They created a simple statement of "Thank you for my message from X, I feel so relieved," followed the process, and let it go.

Cameron focused on the feeling of lightness and relief to hear from that person and knowing everything was okay. They also tried to take away any limiting assumptions they had made, such as "maybe this person doesn't like me." Reading into reasons for silence often creates resistance. Two days after finishing, they received a message from their specific person, and all was well.

We are a collective consciousness and we are all connected. Telepathy and sending people energetic nudges are totally possible!

TRUST THE PROCESS...

As long as you are following your heart, then you cannot fail, only grow. Every day holds a fresh start for you and provides a new opportunity to create happiness on your terms. The Universe delights in you choosing your bliss and believing in yourself.

Try It: Write self-love affirmations or words of intention from your Vision Board on some stickie notes, then pop these on mirrors in your house. That way, you will be continually reminded of where to steer your focus and it gives you an opportunity to speak kindly to yourself in the mirror.

EVERY DAY I'M **FALLING MORE IN LOVE** WITH MYSELF AND MY LIFE, AS I REMEMBER MY TRUTH.

CYCLE 6: COMING HOME

In our last cycle together, we are returning to the fullness of you and knowing you are safe exactly where you are in the here and now. Everything is working out for you and you are so loved. You truly are a wonderful and whole human being. No matter how much inner work or expanding you still feel you need to do, you are enough now—that perfect work in progress, returning to the truth of who you are. You already have so much gold inside you; it's always been there glittering beneath the surface and it deserves to be seen.

Grab your front door key. We're almost home.

INTENTION-SETTING EXERCISE:
PILLOW METHOD

Manifesting includes harnessing the limitless imagination of your childhood when anything was possible. Did you ever put a letter under your pillow for the tooth fairy, saying: "Please take my old tooth in exchange for money"? In the morning, it was so amazing to lift up your pillow and, ta-da!, the money was there! Spoiler alert. It probably wasn't a fairy, but this technique can reconnect you to that nostalgic magic and help support your subconscious programming.

1. Grab a piece of paper and a pen, then create a simple script using the following basic principles:

   - Start with something that you are already grateful for, to put you in the vibration of contentment.

   - Then continue to write your intention statement for your desire: "Thank you, thank you, thank you for [insert your manifestation], which I received with great ease and flow."

   - State how you feel now that you've received what you wanted—for example, "I am so secure/warm/safe/happy."

   - End your script with "And so it is," "Abracadaba," "Amen," or whatever feels right for you.

2. In bed, read your script or say it out loud before you go to sleep, then pop the piece of paper under your pillow. That way, it will be the last thing your mind focuses on, which is powerful for subconscious programming. You don't have to write it out again each night, just repeat the process of reading or saying your script until things manifest and you're ready to start a new one.

3. When the manifestation is under your pillow, you can fall asleep visualizing your life with all the things you have received to support the intention. I am also a huge softy and I love hugging a pillow while I do this because it just makes me feel so much love and good vibes. Go on, you know you want to. Night night, sleep tight!

WEEK 21 INTENTIONS:
MY BODY IS A TEMPLE

You truly are miraculous. According to scientists, the odds of YOU being born are 1 in 400 trillion, maybe even a quadrillion. You are here in this body for a reason, so it's time to treasure it. Think about the following this week:

★ HOW DO YOU WANT TO FEEL?

★ WHAT DO YOU LIKE OR LOVE ABOUT YOUR BODY?

★ WHAT CAN YOUR BODY DO WITHOUT YOU CONSCIOUSLY THINKING ABOUT IT?

★ WHAT ALIGNED ACTIONS WILL SUPPORT YOUR DESIRED FEELINGS AND HELP YOU HONOR YOUR BODY THIS WEEK?

SOUL FOOD FOR THOUGHT

Write a list of 10 positive choices you can make to help you love your body and tick five off that list every day going forward. We can feel under so much pressure to crack all the healthy habits that it becomes unsustainable. Make loving your physical body a realistic commitment for you and build on it, letting your glass feel half-full instead of half-empty.

WEEK 21 FOCUS:
YOUR BODY

Use the three prompts each day to help you appreciate and honor your body— it does so much without you consciously asking it to.

Prompt 1 Express gratitude for your body. So, *"Today, I want to thank _____ for _____"* (for example, my lungs for breathing).

Prompt 2 What is the kindest thing you could do for your body today?

Prompt 3 Plan a self-care treat. So, *"A nourishing, loving choice I could make for my body today is _____"* (for example, dancing, walking, or stretching).

Monday

_____

_____

_____

Tuesday

_____

_____

_____

Wednesday

_____

_____

_____

hursday

_____

_____

_____

riday

_____

_____

_____

Saturday

_____

_____

_____

Sunday

_____

_____

_____

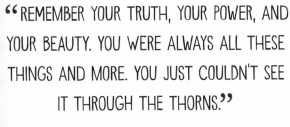 **"REMEMBER YOUR TRUTH, YOUR POWER, AND YOUR BEAUTY. YOU WERE ALWAYS ALL THESE THINGS AND MORE. YOU JUST COULDN'T SEE IT THROUGH THE THORNS."**

WEEK 21 REFLECTIONS

Your physical body is like a car that your spirit has been given to drive in this lifetime. Often, when doing inner soul work, our body focus can go on the back burner. But don't forget your spirit still needs its car. Give yourself regular services! Look back over the last week and think about the following:

Name three blessings, big or small, from this week. How did they make you feel?

1. _____

2. _____

3. _____

How did you love your body this week?

_____

_____

What do you love about being alive and being in your body?

_____

_____

What does your body deserve more of?

_____

_____

How can you listen more to the messages your body is giving to you?

_____

_____

WEEK 22 INTENTIONS:
BE TRUE TO YOU

When you are true to you, you fast-track your expansion because you are living in the fullness of your spirit. As well as speaking your truth, and being honest with yourself about your needs, this also includes living the life you would like and not a life that is expected of you. Think about the following this week:

★ HOW DO YOU WANT TO FEEL?

★ IN WHAT WAYS DO YOU FEEL THAT YOU ARE CURRENTLY "BEING TRUE TO YOU" OR "LIVING AUTHENTICALLY"?

★ IF YOU DIDN'T NEED PERMISSION OR WEREN'T CONCERNED ABOUT THE JUDGMENTS OF OTHERS, IS THERE ANYTHING YOU WOULD DO DIFFERENTLY IN YOUR LIFE?

★ WHAT ALIGNED ACTIONS WILL SUPPORT YOUR DESIRED FEELINGS AND HELP YOU BE TRUE TO YOURSELF THIS WEEK?

SOUL FOOD FOR THOUGHT

Your authenticity and beliefs won't be for everybody and that includes your views on manifestation and healing. That's okay! If you know people in your life who would benefit from the principles in this book, but they aren't open to hearing them, then your job is to lead with love and to show them, through your way of being and how you've created changes. If they're ready, they'll come.

WEEK 22 FOCUS:
AUTHENTICITY

Use the three prompts each day to help you embody authenticity in your life. Remember, you're a multifaceted being with many valid interests and emotions:

Prompt 1 What would you like to reveal today—maybe your vulnerability or humor?

Prompt 2 What is true about you today? Try, *"I am feeling _____"* (for example, kind/beautiful/understanding).

Prompt 3 Affirm with me: *"It's my life! And I have full permission to _____ today"* (for example, be creative/get a tattoo/lay in bed/express my sexuality).

Monday

_____

_____

_____

Tuesday

_____

_____

_____

Wednesday

_____

_____

_____

Thursday

_____

_____

_____

Friday

_____

_____

_____

Saturday

_____

_____

_____

Sunday

_____

_____

_____

"WHEN YOU SHOW UP IN YOUR TRUEST FORM, YOU EMPOWER OTHERS TO DO THE SAME."

WEEK 22 REFLECTIONS

Becoming your future self starts with who you are now. Ask: "What would my future self do?", then show up as them—there's no pretending! Keep going, on small choice at a time. Look back over the last week and think about the followin

Name three blessings, big or small, from this week. How did they make you feel?

1. _____

2. _____

3. _____

How were you "true to you" this week?

_____

_____

In what ways do you think you inspire others?

_____

_____

Are there parts of your body or personality that you're hiding and would like to "let out" more? What could a safe, comfortable first step toward this look like?

_____

_____

Who makes you feel safe enough to be the real you, and why? Tell them if you can!

_____

_____

WEEK 23 INTENTIONS:
EXPRESS YOURSELF!

doesn't get much airtime spiritually, but your self-expression and style are big parts of your point of attraction. When you show up confidently in your power, your aura is so magnetic. Anything that adds to you and magnifies your energy is a bonus. Think about the following this week:

★ HOW DO YOU WANT TO FEEL?

★ HOW WOULD YOU DESCRIBE YOUR PERSONAL SENSE OF STYLE?

★ WHAT ENERGY WOULD YOU LIKE TO CONVEY WITH YOUR STYLE OR SELF-EXPRESSION? PERHAPS THERE'S SOMETHING BOLD AND NEW YOU WOULD LIKE TO TRY?

★ WHAT ALIGNED ACTIONS WILL SUPPORT YOUR DESIRED FEELINGS AND HELP YOU SHOW UP AS YOUR MOST CONFIDENT SELF?

SOUL FOOD FOR THOUGHT

If you're calling in a new career—or you want more clients or romantic dates—how would you dress when living that reality? There is a concept in manifesting called "acting as if" (or behaving as you would if it was already yours). Don't wait until you've got the job to dress nicely. Ditch the joggers and put out that signal of "I'm here and I am ready!".

WEEK 23 FOCUS:
SELF-EXPRESSION

Use the three prompts each day to inspire you to express yourself fully and celebrate who you are:

Prompt 1 Pick something from your wardrobe or styling toolkit: what do you love about this and how does it support your feelings?

Prompt 2 Whose confidence or style inspires you? Tell them if you can.

Prompt 3 What self-expression choice would make you feel confident today— a lipstick, earrings, or *that* pair of shoes? Perhaps even walking taller.

Monday

Tuesday

Wednesday

Thursday

_____

_____

_____

Friday

_____

_____

_____

Saturday

_____

_____

_____

Sunday

_____

_____

_____

"EVERY DAY THAT WE LIVE AND BREATHE IS A
SPECIAL OCCASION, SO EVERY DAY CAN BE A TIME
TO SPARKLE AND SHINE BRIGHTLY."

WEEK 23 REFLECTIONS

Often what we admire in someone else is what we're seeking in ourselves. By considering who or what inspires us, we can work out what we value and what we're reaching for. Look back over the last week and think about the following

Name three blessings, big or small, from this week. How did they make you feel

1. _____

2. _____

3. _____

How did dressing and expressing your power make you feel this week?

_____

_____

What's the nicest thing a stranger has ever said to you? How did it make you fee

_____

_____

How would you like to describe yourself in the future?

_____

_____

Is there anything you need to say to your inner child who perhaps didn't have the confidence or permission to be themselves?

_____

_____

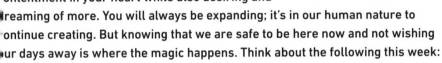

WEEK 24 INTENTIONS:
MANIFESTING HAPPINESS

It is entirely possible to hold happiness and contentment in your heart while also desiring and dreaming of more. You will always be expanding; it's in our human nature to continue creating. But knowing that we are safe to be here now and not wishing our days away is where the magic happens. Think about the following this week:

★ HOW DO YOU WANT TO FEEL?

★ WHAT OR WHO HAS MADE YOU HAPPIEST LATELY, AND WHY? HINT: IT MAY EVEN BE YOURSELF!

★ CLOSE YOUR EYES AND VISUALIZE YOUR PERFECT DAY FROM START TO FINISH—WHO IS IN IT, WHAT ARE YOU DOING, WHERE ARE YOU? HOW DOES IT FEEL AND HOW CAN YOU CREATE MORE OF THIS?

★ WHAT ALIGNED ACTIONS WILL SUPPORT YOUR DESIRED FEELINGS AND HELP YOU PRIORITIZE YOUR HAPPINESS?

SOUL FOOD FOR THOUGHT

It's okay to destabilize in order to find a new balance. Sometimes we have to take something apart to rebuild it better than the original. Change, although scary, can be a necessary and positive thing as it propels you toward new places, people, and passions.

WEEK 24 FOCUS:
CONTENTMENT

Use the three prompts each day to help you connect to feelings of joy in your life and remember times when you were happy in the past:

Prompt 1 Start your day positively by thinking of a happy memory. How does this feel and what does it teach you (if anything)?

Prompt 2 Name one thing you are happy and satisfied with today?

Prompt 3 What would light you up today—maybe your favorite childhood movie?

Monday

_____

_____

_____

Tuesday

_____

_____

_____

Wednesday

_____

_____

_____

Thursday

_____

_____

_____

Friday

_____

_____

_____

Saturday

_____

_____

_____

Sunday

_____

_____

_____

"WE CAN ENJOY THE FLEETING MAGIC OF THE RAINBOW WITHOUT NEEDING TO CHASE THE POT OF GOLD. THERE IS VALUE IN WHAT IT IS AND NOT JUST IN ITS POTENTIAL."

WEEK 24 REFLECTIONS

Remember that while happiness is what we are reaching for, we must always make time and space for other emotions. Know you are also worthy on your darkest days and that your tears carry no shame. You can still believe in your creation while experiencing your humanity.

Name three blessings, big or small, from this week. How did they make you feel?

1. _____

2. _____

3. _____

What or who made you smile this week?

_____

_____

Why is your happiness a top priority for you?

_____

_____

At this point in your journey, what does happiness mean to you?

_____

_____

What could your happy-ever-after look like?

_____

_____

SUCCESS STORIES
SAM/CONNIE/ARNA

Sam used the *Pillow Method* (see page 118) to manifest a car. He really didn't have much money, and within days of writing his statement his nextdoor neighbors put their car up for sale for the exact amount of money he could afford.

Using the *Scripting* method (see page 58), **Connie** manifested a new home. She and her partner didn't have the funds, but she was looking at a house online and saying how nice it would be. Completely unexpectedly, his family said they would like to support them and made their dreams come true. She was overwhelmed by how fast it all happened and how blessed she felt. They're still living there now!

And **Arna** manifested her dream job by using the clarity work exercise (see page 10) and doing EFT tapping (see page 136), harnessing all her incredible skills. Out of the blue she received a call, as she had been recommended for a role by a previous employer. And just like that, she manifested her career goals.

Remember, solutions can always be fast, effortless, and close at hand!

TRUST THE PROCESS...

Don't wait for someone to believe in you before you believe in yourself. If you wanted a record deal, would you say: "I won't make any music until I get the deal because only then will I know I am good enough"? Of course not, how can you get the deal without shining brightly first? Show up, create, do what you love, be yourself, and amazing things will follow. It's your time.

POWER TOOLS TO USE

To support your subconscious programming, healing, and expansion I am providing you with three bonus tools to help you shift your point of attraction. Full instructions are included with each video at: www.missmanifesther.com/manifestinghappiness

Tool 1: Emotional Freedom Technique

EFT (Emotional Freedom Technique) Tapping is a holistic energy healing practice that can also be used as a self-help tool, allowing us to regulate our emotions quickly and efficiently. It has many uses, including reducing anxiety ahead of job interviews or exams, releasing limiting beliefs around money, and even helping with pain management. It has been shown that the benefits are endless.

EFT tapping on a series of meridian points has been shown to reduce stress and have a significant effect on the amygdala, which is the primitive part of the brain related to the fight-or-flight response. In this EFT sequence I give you an all-inclusive tapping for happiness, which covers bases such as gratitude, self-worth, trusting the process, and that all you want is possible. It's on the way!

Tool 2: Guided Visualization

Visualization, as we learned when making a Vision Board (see page 18), can trick the subconscious mind into believing we are experiencing what we're visualizing right now, and it instructs the subconscious on what we value as important and what to focus on creating.

In this guided visualization, which supports some of the manifestation techniques outlined in this book, I take you on a journey to see all you want to create in the future and to connect to the desired feelings that you want to experience from these things. In feeling these now, we can call more of them into our lives. From there, we also gain clarity on labeling the feelings that we want to focus on, so generating more of these in our reality.

Tool 3: Subliminals

Subliminals are audio tracks containing hidden affirmations which may be played at the level of a whisper, sped up, or turned down so they are completely undetectable. The affirmations bypass the conscious mind and go straight to programming the subconscious mind.

Your subconscious mind accepts what you tell it repeatedly and because it is like a computer program running your show, these subliminal tracks are super powerful for changing your code! I like to call them "the lazy way of manifesting" because in changing the program, your magnetism shifts. You can show up with new behaviors, beliefs, and energy. The beauty of this is that you just need to pop subliminals on and fall asleep to them.

There are many subliminals suitable for a variety topics such as body changes, attracting customers, or manifesting a partner. For you I have created a contentment and magnetic attraction subliminal to help you find your peace in the here and now and to attract in blessings, opportunities, and more reasons to feel happy!

"I AM THE MARVELOUS MAGNET FOR MANIFESTATIONS AND MIRACLES."

YOUR SIX-MONTH REVIEW

Pass me the tissues, as it's almost time to say goodbye. But this isn't really goodbye, it's "I'll see you later." I have been cheering you on from afar and I celebrate you for honoring yourself and choosing the road to happiness every day through our reflective practices together.

I am so grateful that you chose to pick up this book and to trust it to hold space for your expansion. It takes commitment and self-love to consistently put time into your healing and happiness, especially when the growing gets tough, but somewhere inside you knew you were worthy of this investment. So, to acknowledge how far you've come, to see your existing magic and enough-ness, let's take time to review the last six months and to set some intentions for your next chapter. Grab a notepad and answer the questions on the following topics:

You're manifesting all the time!

1. Take a look at your Vision Board from Cycle 1 (see page 18). Which things and feelings have manifested from your board? In what ways have you channeled focus into your intentions along the way?

2. What are five of your favorite manifestations or blessings that you've received over the last six months, and why? Tell the stories of how they unfolded in your life in your notebook.

3. What came to you most easily over the last six months?

4. Were those manifestations specific or based on feeling? Or both? What does that teach you about the process?

5. What have you learned the most about manifestation so far and what more would you like to learn?

Celebrate your successes on the journey, not just at the finish line

1. What were your greatest successes or achievements in the last six months?

2. In what areas of your life do you feel most abundant, and why?

3. What empowering beliefs do you hold around attracting money? This could involve where money can come from or how there's enough for everyone.

4. What empowering beliefs do you have about your career? They could relate to your abilities or the options available to you.

5. In what ways would you like to celebrate your successes more? What could feel rewarding at each milestone?

Love makes the world go round

1. Who are you so thankful to have in your life right now and why do you value them?

2. In what ways have you felt loved and supported by other people over the last six months?

3. In what ways have you lit up the lives of others over the last six months?

4. Who have you loved spending time with the most, and why? What does good company mean to you?

5. In what ways have you found new love and appreciation for yourself? See yourself with softer eyes.

Wheel of Life

Lastly, bearing all your answers in mind, let's revisit your Wheel of Life (see page 13). Copy the topics from your first wheel and write them in the new blank wheel on the next page. Then grab your coloring pens, rate how full you feel for each topic, and fill in the segments again. Now do the following:

1. Compare your current wheel with your wheel from six months ago. In which categories are you feeling more fulfilled, and why?

2. Who were you when you started this journal? Describe where you were in terms of feelings, situations, and so on.

3. What have been your greatest lessons over the last six months? These could be about yourself or about life or your relationships.

4. Who are you today as you get ready to close this journal? Describe your feelings, any life changes, and your potential.

5. Zoom out. When you look at all your responses for this review so far, how do you feel emotionally and in your body?

Date: _____

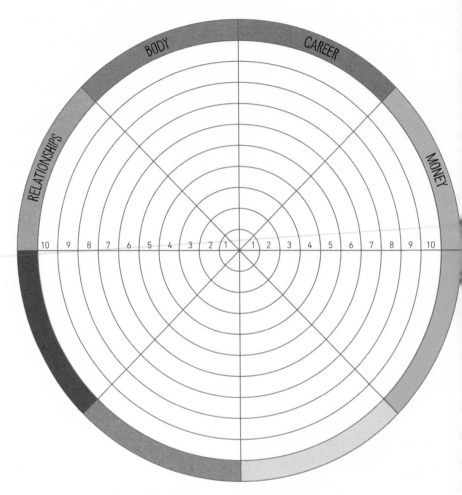

Scores:

Relationships [   ]   _____ [   ]

Body [   ]   _____ [   ]

Career [   ]   _____ [   ]

Money [   ]   _____ [   ]

The next stepping stones

1. Where does happiness, contentment, and satisfaction already exist in your life?

2. How can you continue to nurture what is already wonderful? Remember, what you focus on multiplies!

3. Are there any life areas or beliefs you would still like to work on that will support your happiness? What could the first steps look like?

4. If you could create four intention affirmations for your next chapter, what would they be? Write them in the spaces below:

    I am ready to/for_____in my life.

    I choose_____for myself.

    I get to focus on_____

    I am allowing and welcoming the feelings of_____ to flow into my experience.

5. Now write yourself a self-love note here:

'Dear _____

I am so proud of you because_____

I promise to_____

You are worthy of_____because_____

Your heart is_____

You have permission to_____

And on your down days, I want you to remember you are _____

You are attracting_____

Manifesting is real because_____

So your happiness is inevitable.

I love you."

GLOSSARY

Abundance A feeling that life is overflowing and filled with a very large quantity of something, such as money, love, or friends.

Affirmation A declaration or simple statement of what you want to be or what you are attracting—for example: "I am beautiful."

Aligned action Taking a feel-good action, ideally from a place of inspiration. In your body, this feels more like an "I get to" than an "I should do."

Being in resistance Having thoughts, feelings, or beliefs that hold you back from creating the life you want. Your body will often feel tense or you will struggle to trust and enjoy *living in the end*.

Detachment Feeling able to let go of what you desire, knowing you will be okay without this.

Earth angel A wonderful human being who has a desire to love, support, and help others. They often feel heaven-sent in a difficult moment.

Energy Everything is energy, including us. We all have an unseen energy field influenced by our emotions, thought patterns, feelings, and actions. This means we vibrate at a certain frequency, which affects our *point of attraction*. Often called vibration or frequency.

Law of Attraction The universal law or concept that whatever you focus your energy on will come back to you. Popularized by Abraham Hicks.

Living in the end This means living in a place of faith and trust, and acting as if what you want is on its way or here now, without trying to problem solve or push a solution.

Patch of contrast This is a time in your life that is showing you the things you don't want. It can give you greater clarity regarding what you truly desire.

Point of attraction You are a magnet and technically the center of your own universe. This means you are an energy source that draws things toward you or pushes them away based on what you emit energetically.

Pivot In a negative or challenging situation, to be able to turn your thoughts around and focus on something more positive, uplifting, or productive in order to shift your energy.

Quantum jumping or shifting When a belief system radically changes who you are at a core level. Since we manifest from the inside out, this unlocks new potentials in our reality that were previously unavailable. This can create rapid changes in your 3D reality.

Reacting to the 3D This is to be avoided—don't allow what is going on around you to influence your faith or belief in your manifestation coming through.

Self-concept Your idea of your own identity and who you are, which is drawn from the collective beliefs that you hold about yourself. These beliefs can be conscious or subconscious.

Source/Universe/God/Divine Love A sense of a higher power that is all-loving and to which everyone and everything is connected.

Upleveling You have progressed and evolved in a certain area and life is getting better for you as a result.

Vision board A collection of pictures and words or phrases that sum up your dream life. Usually added to a piece of paper, corkboard or digital collage.

Visualization To imagine and see something as an image in your mind. Ideally, this allows you to connect to the feeling of experiencing right now.

RESOURCES

Below are some ideas for further reading and useful websites to assist you on your manifesting journey:

Esther McCann

www.missmanifesther.com

www.youtube.com/c/missmanifesther

www.instagram.com/missmanifesther

Abraham Hicks

Ask and It is Given: Learning to Manifest Your Desires, Hay House, 2004

www.abraham-hicks.com

Amanda Frances

Rich as F*ck: More Money Than You Know What to Do With, Amanda Frances Inc., 2020

www.amandafrances.com

Dr Joe Dispenza

Becoming Supernatural, Hay House, 2017

www.drjoedispenza.com

Dr Wayne Dyer

The Power of Intention: Learning to Co-Create Your World Your Way, Hay House, 2004

www.drwaynedyer.com

Gabrielle Bernstein

Judgement Detox: Release the Beliefs That Hold You Back from Living a Better Life, Hay House, 2018

Super Attractor: Methods for Manifesting A Life Beyond Your Wildest Dreams, Hay House, 2019

The Universe Has Your Back: How to Feel Safe and Trust Your Life No Matter What, Hay House, 2016

www.gabbybernstein.com

Giselle La Pompe-Moore

Take It In: Do the Inner Work, Create Your Best Damn Life, Penguin Audiobook, 2022

www.gisellelpm.com

Louise Hay

You Can Heal Your Life Companion Book, Hay House, 2004

Mirror Work, Hay House, 2016

www.louisehay.com

Napoleon Hill

Think and Grow Rich, Chump Change, 1937

www.naphill.org

Neville Goddard

Infinite Potential: The Greatest Works of Neville Goddard, St. Martin's Essentials, 2019

Rhonda Byrne

The Secret Series, especially *The Magic*, Simon & Schuster, 2012

www.thesecret.tv

Vex King

Good Vibes, Good Life: How Self-Love is the Key to Unlocking Your Greatness, Hay House, 2018

www.vexking.com

A FINAL THOUGHT

Manifesting happiness was never about getting the stuff or placing all your power in a tool. Rather it was always to do with remembering your magnetic power within and your ability to create and attract, just by being in the fullness of you. You were always enough and joy is always available to you now. Even in the smallest of things.

So remember, this is not the end.

It is just the beginning.

ABOUT THE AUTHOR

Esther McCann, who is also known as Miss Manifesther, is a manifestation coach and spiritual mentor. She helps people to manifest success, love, and fulfillment on their terms through manifestation principles, mindset coaching, and energy work. As a result, her clients become magnetic masters of their energy, release their subconscious resistance to success, and achieve their goals from a place of alignment. Esther is also a qualified management and life coach, as well as a practitioner of Emotional Freedom Technique and other holistic modalities.

AUTHOR'S ACKNOWLEDGMENTS

I'd like to take this opportunity to thank everybody who has helped in making this book become a reality, and for believing in me to be able to deliver it to the world. Thank you to everyone on the team at Dorling Kindersley for all your hard work in bringing this together. Especially Jo Lightfoot, Pete Jorgensen, Florence Ward, Caroline West, and Joelle Wheelwright. Thank you also to Kerrie McNeill for all your beautiful illustrations that help bring the magic of this journal to life.

Thank you to Laura McKeown, my soul sister, who I just couldn't be without. Thank you for continually being my sounding board for all the content and for your continuing wisdom and friendship. Thank you additionally to Arna Van Goch for being one of my biggest cheerleaders when this was taking flight—you are always a grounding spirit in which I can trust.

In the year of writing this I was truly reminded of all my incredible friendships and how supported I am by the most wonderful connections, and I am so grateful to serve the most beautiful clients. There are too many names to list but to anybody who has been by my side at any point in my journey, your presence has touched my life. Thank you.